Concepts in the Social Sciences

# Democracy

## Third Edition

*Anthony Arblaster*

**Open University Press**
*Buckingham · Philadelphia*

Open University Press
Celtic Court
22 Ballmoor
Buckingham
MK18 1XW

email: enquiries@openup.co.uk
world wide web: www.openup.co.uk

and
325 Chestnut Street
Philadelphia, PA 19106, USA

First published 1987
Reprinted 1991, 1993

Second edition first published 1994
Reprinted 1996, 1999, 2001

Third edition published 2002

A catalogue record of this book is available from the British Library

ISBN 0 335 20969 6 (pb)    0 335 20970 X (hb)

**Library of Congress Cataloging-in-Publication Data**
Arblaster, Anthony.
    Democracy/Anthony Arblaster. – 3rd ed.
        p. cm. – (Concepts in the social sciences)
    Includes bibliographical references and index.
    ISBN 0-335-20970-X – ISBN 0-335-20969-6 (pbk.)
    1. Democracy.   I. Title.   II. Series.
JC423.A685 2002
321.8–dc21                                          2002023853

Typeset by Type Study, Scarborough
Printed and bound in Great Britain by
Marston Book Services Limited, Oxford

# Democracy

Current Titles

| Democracy (Third Edition) | Anthony Arblaster |
| Discrimination | Michael Banton |
| Citizenship | J.M. Barbalet |
| Welfare (Second Edition) | Norman Barry |
| Freedom | Zygmunt Bauman |
| Bureaucracy (Second Edition) | David Beetham |
| Nationalism | Craig Calhoun |
| Trotskyism | Alex Callinicos |
| Revolution and Counter-revolution | Peter Calvert |
| Policy (Second Edition) | H.K. Colebatch |
| Socialism | Bernard Crick |
| Exchange | John Davis |
| Social Science | Gerard Delanty |
| Social Darwinism | Peter Dickens |
| Power | Keith Dowding |
| Rights | Michael Freeden |
| Feminism | Jane Freedman |
| Science | Steve Fuller |
| Liberalism (Second Edition) | John Gray |
| The State | John A. Hall and G. John Ikenberry |
| Kinship | C.C. Harris |
| Sovereignty | John Hoffman |
| Discourse | David Howarth |
| Utopianism | Krishan Kumar |
| Social Structure | José López and John Scott |
| Postmodernity (Second Edition) | David Lyon |
| Ideology (Second Edition) | David McLellan |
| Pluralism | Gregor McLennan |
| Fascism | Mark Neocleous |
| Conservatism | Robert Nisbet |
| Structuration | John Parker |
| Race and Ethnicity | John Rex |
| Postcommunism | Richard Sakwa |
| Orientalism | Ziauddin Sardar |
| Capitalism | Peter Saunders |
| Class | Richard Scase |
| Caste | Ursula Sharma |
| Ecologism | Mark J. Smith |
| Culture | Mark J. Smith |
| Populism | Paul Taggart |
| Status | Bryan S. Turner |
| Multiculturalism | C.W. Watson |

# Contents

*Preface and Acknowledgements*                              vii
*Preface to the Third Edition*                             viii

1   Introduction: Defining Democracy                          1

PART ONE: HISTORY

2   The Invention of Democracy                               15

3   The Re-emergence of Democracy                            26

4   Popular Politics                                         37

PART TWO: IDEAS

5   Government by the People                                 59

6   Majority Rule and its Problems                           66

7   Equality and the General Interest                        72

8   Representation and 'Direct' Democracy                    79

9   Consent, Freedom and Debate                              86

10 - Conclusion: Creating Democracy                          95

*Notes*                                                     109
*Bibliography*                                              116
*Index*                                                     120

# Preface and Acknowledgements

Lurking here and there in the backwoods of the social studies, or 'sciences', there are no doubt still a few old-fashioned positivists who believe that you can 'keep politics out of politics'; who suppose, in other words, that you can, or should try to, write a book about democracy as 'objectively' as one might write about the mating habits of goldfish or the geology of the moon. It is more difficult than the positivists suppose to be 'objective' even about goldfish or geology. What possibility, then, is there of writing with cold detachment about something which matters to us all as much as democracy? And even if there were, would it really be desirable? Neutrality in such matters is all too likely to be a recipe for dullness.

It seemed better to run the risk of annoying readers rather than boring them. I have therefore not tried to avoid being controversial in this book, which is better regarded as one more contribution to an ongoing debate than as an attempt at anything more magisterial. I hope, however, that it will prove useful to students (in the widest sense of that word) of political ideas and ideologies. If it stimulates a little discussion among them it will, I think, have served its purpose.

In preparing and writing this book I made extensive use of the resources of Sheffield University Library, for which I am most grateful. My friend and colleague Geraint Williams kindly read the chapter on Greek democracy and made several useful suggestions and necessary corrections. I am grateful to Frank Parkin, editor of this series of books, for his encouragement and support. Above all, I must thank my wife Lynda for help in preparing the original manuscript for publication, as well as both its revised versions.

Anthony Arblaster
Sheffield, January 2002

# Preface to the Third Edition

This book was first published in 1987, in the last years of the Cold War between the Soviet Union and the West. Since then, the global political context in which democracy has to be considered, both as theory and practice, has changed swiftly and dramatically. The collapse of European Communism, together with the disintegration of dictatorships and authoritarian systems in the Philippines, Chile, South Africa and elsewhere, engendered an atmosphere of triumphalism in the West, in which it was claimed that there was no alternative ideology to rival the seemingly unstoppable spread of capitalist democracy.

This rather complacent mood did not last long, however. On the one hand, Western political and social values faced a renewed challenge from militant Islam. On the other, globalization, and the ever-growing wealth and power of vast transnational conglomerates, several of which are wealthier than the poorest nation-states, posed a different kind of threat to the principle of elected and accountable government. If the power of democratic governments was dwarfed by these unelected and largely unaccountable corporations, did that not tend to discredit democracy itself? And if we also saw forms of government developing at the transnational level, in the European Union for example, was there not then a need to develop democratic procedures at that level also? The practice of democracy seemed to be lagging behind the realities of political and economic power.

It is these kinds of developments, rather than any striking advances in theorizing about democracy, that have led me to make some quite substantial revisions to the text of the earlier editions of this book. Its basic structure remains the same, but the emphasis has shifted to take account of recent changes, and the final chapter in particular has been expanded. Today the future of democracy looks more complex and uncertain than perhaps it did in the later years of the twentieth century.

Anthony Arblaster
Sheffield, January 2002

# Introduction: Defining Democracy

At first sight, it might appear that to produce a book about democracy at the beginning of the twenty-first century would be to do no more than add one further voice to the chorus of self-congratulatory celebration which has drowned out most of the more uncertain or sceptical utterances, at least in the West, since the abrupt and generally unexpected collapse of European Communism and its global superpower, the Soviet Union, in the years from 1989 to 1991. The West is in the ascendant. Democracy defeated totalitarianism. Capitalism finally and definitively proved its superiority to Communism as an economic system. What room was there left for doubt or argument?

This triumphalist interpretation of the recent past was supported, in a more philosophical vein, by the historicist arguments of Francis Fukuyama, a former US State Department official whose article, 'The End of History', appeared with extraordinary timeliness early in 1989. He then developed the argument at book length, and, in the wake of the attacks on New York and Washington in 2001, he reaffirmed his conviction that his interpretation of nineteenth- and twentieth-century historical evolution remains valid.[1] Fukuyama's suggestion was that capitalist democracy represents the final and highest stage of the development of human political and economic institutions. Capitalist democracy has not yet been realized on a global scale, and perhaps may never be; but nevertheless that is the goal to which all developing and modernizing societies tend to aspire, however fiercely the tendency may be resisted by reactionaries and religious fundamentalists on the one hand, and socialists and Communists on the other.

Such a historical perspective was clearly designed as an alternative to the Marxist one. That envisages capitalism and bourgeois democracy as interim developments which will eventually be superseded by socialism and the end of government and the state as we know them: 'The government of persons will be replaced by the administration of things.' Fukuyama's thesis was thus an audacious one, which might well have been received as a suggestive *jeu d'esprit*, had not events suddenly offered such dramatic evidence of the instability and indeed transience of institutionalized Communism, while simultaneously seeming to demonstrate both the durability and the attractiveness of democracy with capitalism as a combined politico-economic system.

The Western world has always tended to be complacent about democracy. It has long been assumed that democracy is something which already exists in our part of the world. (Fukuyama included in his book a chart which classified Great Britain, the United States and several other countries as 'liberal democracies' as long ago as 1848, even though well over half the population in Great Britain and the United States was disenfranchised at the time, and slavery was not yet abolished in the United States.[2]) In the past century democracy had to be defended, against fascism before 1945 and against Communism during the Cold War. But both threats have now vanished, or diminished to the point of insignificance. The major task which now confronts the democracies is to help establish democratic systems and institutions in societies which have never known them, or where they were swept away by authoritarian takeovers. How much has actually been done by the West to promote the growth of democracy is a question to which we will return later.

This perspective on democracy starts from the assumption that democracy is something which 'we' (in the West) already have, but are generously and idealistically anxious to export to less fortunate parts of the globe. To give an account of democracy will therefore be largely an exercise in description of current Western realities, coupled, perhaps, with some account of how this happy state of affairs came about. Such an account will not have to be either critical or challenging, although it may be found to be so in societies where democracy has yet to be realized. The disappearance of the 'people's democracies' of the Communist world has only reinforced this self-satisfied mood; for however grotesque a mockery Communist and Marxist societies made of the democratic idea, there were traces in their theory, and perhaps even in some of their practice, of an alternative conception of what democracy might mean which did offer some kind of a challenge to Western complacency. C.B. Macpherson gave a sympathetic account of these alternative perspectives in *The Real World of Democracy*.[3]

Yet as soon as we start thinking seriously about what democracy is, what the term means, and has meant, some healthy doubts will begin to cloud this mood of self-congratulation. For democracy is a concept before it is a fact, and because it is a concept it has no single precise and agreed meaning. It has had very different meanings and connotations in its long history, and is understood differently today in the context of different social and economic systems. What is now called democracy in the West would not satisfy some of those, past and present, who have had a different conception of it.

Common sense may want to brush this aside as an unnecessarily sophisticated attempt to confuse the issue. 'We all know', it might be briskly claimed, 'which nations or states are democratic and which are not.' But do we? For instance: is the test of a democracy the fact that a government is elected by the votes of the people? When Hitler became Chancellor of Germany in 1933, he did so through a normal constitutional process, and as leader of the party with the largest single share of the popular vote in elections for the Reichstag. The Nazi Party received 43.9 per cent of the vote – almost exactly the percentage vote gained by the Conservatives in Britain under Margaret Thatcher in 1983 and 1987, and by Labour in 1997 and 2001. Few people in Britain have quarrelled with the legitimacy of governments which obtain less than half the votes cast. So Hitler had a good democratic claim to govern Germany after March 1933. Yet no one would want to describe the Third Reich as a democracy. So at what point did it cease to be so?

Elections of a kind used to be held in the Soviet Union and in other Communist countries, and in many other countries which are, officially or unofficially, one-party states. Many people would not want to call these states democratic either. They would claim that elections in the Soviet Union, or in, say, Egypt today, or the Philippines under President Marcos, were not free: the people did not have a genuine choice open to them. But what constitutes a free election? There were elections in Nicaragua in 1984, contested by a plurality of parties, several opposed to the Sandinista government. Nicaragua contended that the elections were free, and that they demonstrated that the Sandinista government had genuine popular support. The United States, and some other Western governments, went to considerable lengths to try and discredit these elections as being not free, but fraudulent. So was Nicaragua then a democracy, or did it only become so when the Sandinistas lost the elections of 1990, as some would argue?

Or take contemporary Britain. One common conception of democracy is that it means 'government by the people', or at least by the people's elected representatives – since it is generally accepted, rightly or wrongly, that in large modern states the people themselves cannot govern. But since 'the people' are likely to be divided among themselves, the government is likely to be representative, not of all the people, but at best of a majority of them. Already, then, we are having to redefine democracy. In practice it means government by the representatives of a majority of the people. But Britain, which is usually thought of as a democracy, especially by the British, does not meet even that criterion. No British government since the attainment of adult suffrage, other than coalitions, has been elected with even a bare majority of the votes cast. With an electoral system like Britain's, and with more than two parties sharing the popular vote, a government is elected by, and so represents, only the single largest minority of those who vote. This may not be much more than 40 per cent of the voters, leaving the non-voters and the remaining 60 per cent of those who took part in the election to be governed by an administration which is not of their choosing. We are already at quite a distance from the original simple idea of government by the people.

And there are, of course, other grounds for doubt. To what extent do the elected representatives of the people, that is the House of Commons, actually govern? (We will leave aside, for the moment, the upper house of the British Parliament, which still consists entirely of persons elected by nobody at all.) If, as is generally agreed, it is not Parliament itself which governs, to what extent is the government itself – ministers, civil servants, and the whole apparatus of the state – actually accountable and answerable to the Commons, and so in principle controllable by it? It is well known that many Members of Parliament are among those who are deeply dissatisfied with Parliament's ability to control the executive, or even to find out what it is doing. How is it possible, in a democracy, for a committee of the House of Commons to find itself prevented from interviewing civil servants when it wishes to do so, or to be faced with witnesses who refuse to answer questions that are put to them, as was the case when the Commons Select Committee on Defence attempted to investigate the Westland affair in 1986? Why did it need a judicial inquiry under Lord Justice Scott to uncover the truth about Britain's supply of arms to Iraq before the Gulf War of 1991, and to uncover the extent to which government ministers gave misleading or untruthful answers to parliamentary questions at the time?

We do not need to reach firm answers to these questions to see that the realities of British politics – both the process of electing a parliament and the relation of that elected body to those who actually form and control the machinery of state – certainly do not neatly correspond to or embody the original notion of government by the people or the people's representatives. Is this the best that can be achieved, the nearest practicable approximation to the democratic principle? Or is there not ample room for improvement? And if the latter is the case, is it not at least something of an oversimplification to say that Britain is a democracy, as if the problematic relationship of British realities to the basic democratic principle or ideal can be simply ignored or brushed aside?

Or take one province of Great Britain: Northern Ireland. For 50 years between 1922 and 1972 the Unionist Party won every election in the province with a clear majority of the votes cast. Unscrupulous manipulation of constituency boundaries gave them even more of the seats in the Stormont Parliament than they properly deserved, but this gerrymandering was unnecessary. Even without it the Unionists had a popular mandate such as no Westminster government has enjoyed. They used this strong position to reduce the Catholic and generally Irish nationalist minority of the population to the level of second-class citizens, discriminated against in public housing and employment, and excluded from positions of power and authority. In doing this they undoubtedly commanded the enthusiastic approval of most of their Protestant supporters. Was this, then, democracy in action in Northern Ireland? Certainly, when Unionist leaders call for a 'return to democracy' in the province, that is what they have in mind – the restoration of simple majority rule, which would in effect be the restoration of Protestant domination. It is easy to say that the years of Unionist rule were a travesty of what democracy is, or ought to be. But what, precisely, is the theoretical basis for denying it the honorific title of 'democracy'? If democracy does not mean the rule of the majority, what does it mean?

Here, surely, are sufficient examples to show that, however banal or simple our definition of democracy, it soon turns out that it cannot be used as a plain, uncomplicated term of description at all. As soon as we start thinking seriously about what democracy means, and what the relation is between the idea and the reality, we discover that common sense is a quite inadequate guide.

And the problem of the relation between idea and reality is only one of the difficulties. Just because contemporary reality does not readily correspond to some of the classical notions of what democracy is, some twentieth-century writers argued that we need to revise our conception of democracy itself, to suit what is realistically possible in modern advanced societies. We do not have to follow them along that particular path to see that the question of definition is also raised by the examples I have briefly cited. Those who are unhappy about calling Unionist Northern Ireland a democracy, or equally unhappy about not calling Britain as a whole a democracy, are compelled to return to questions of meaning and definition. Attention to the theory of democracy cannot honestly be avoided. We need to be clearer than we usually are about what we mean by 'democracy'. And as soon as we begin to enquire into the meaning of the term, we discover that it has been and still is understood in a variety of different ways, which may have a common core or root but are not identical.

This is not a matter of accident, or simple confusion, or even of deliberate attempts to use or misuse the word for particular political purposes – although all of these factors may, and in fact do, come into it. Democracy is what W.B. Gallie once christened an 'essentially contestable concept'. It is an inherently debatable and changeable idea. Like 'freedom', 'equality', 'justice', 'human rights', and so forth, 'democracy' is a term which, whatever its precise meaning, will always signify for many a cherished political principle or ideal, and for that reason alone it is never likely to achieve a single agreed meaning. This is inconvenient to the tidy-minded, but should not otherwise be a matter for regret. Democracy is one of the most durable ideas in politics, and it became, in the twentieth century, one of the most central. It is not likely to lose that centrality, but nor is its meaning likely to become static or fixed. Neither lexicographers nor political theorists can or should hope to halt this process of constant revision, although they may legitimately aspire to guide or nudge it in one direction rather than another.

There are therefore good reasons to think that those who try to define democracy only in terms of present-day realities – as a type of political system or culture which some societies possess and others do not – will find themselves left behind by history. Democracy is likely to remain not only a contestable concept, but also a 'critical' concept: that is, a norm or ideal by which reality is tested and found wanting. There will always be some further extension or growth of democracy to be undertaken. That is not to say that a perfect democracy is in the end attainable, any more than is perfect freedom or perfect justice. It is rather that the idea and ideal are always potentially a corrective, rather than a prop, to complacency.

In saying this, I am saying little more than that history, more or less as we have known it, will continue in the future (if humanity has a future). For when we look backwards, it is this process of constant change and adaptation in ideas as well as material realities that we discover. To suppose that the definition of democracy can ever be fixed, or, even more arrogantly, that democracy has been or will be definitively realized at some point during the twenty-first century, is to be blind not only to the probabilities of the future but also to our knowledge of the past. Hence any study of what democracy is, any attempt to discover its essence or meaning, must necessarily be a historical study at least in part. Contemporary understanding of the idea needs to refer to historical usage of the term, if only to prevent an acceptance, without doubt or enquiry, of present notions of democracy as permanently definitive.

A historical perspective reveals, in particular, one at first sight rather puzzling and paradoxical feature of the history of democracy. For most of its long history, from the classical Greeks to the present day, democracy was seen by the enlightened and educated as one of the worst types of government and society imaginable. Democracy was more or less synonymous with 'the rule of the mob', and was, by definition, a threat to all the central values of a civilized and orderly society. C.B. Macpherson puts this point very well:

> Democracy used to be a bad word. Everybody who was anybody knew that democracy, in its original sense of rule by the people or government in accordance with the will of the bulk of the people, would be a bad thing – fatal to individual freedom and to all the graces of civilized living. That was the position taken by pretty nearly all men of intelligence from the earliest historical times down to about a hundred years ago. Then, within fifty years, democracy became a good thing.[4]

Clearly it is of prime importance to know how and why this dramatic reversal of traditional attitudes has occurred, and to ask ourselves why our approval of democracy should be so automatic and unhesitating when, had we been born a century or so earlier, we would have been equally unhesitating in disclaiming any support for so dangerous and radical a notion. Such a rapid and drastic change in attitudes arouses suspicion. Have popular attitudes towards democracy changed so dramatically? Or has democracy itself been adapted to accommodate earlier suspicions and hostility?

We may get a clue to a possible answer from the following exchange in *Waste*, by Harley Granville-Barker, a play set in the milieu of the British governing class in the early twentieth century:

> BLACKBOROUGH: ... the statesman's task is the accommodation of stubborn fact to shifting circumstance ... and in effect to the practical capacities of the average stupid man. Democracy involves the admission of that.
>
> LADY JULIA (*whose patience is being tried*): I am at least not a democrat, Mr Blackborough.
>
> BLACKBOROUGH: Nor I ... more of a democrat than I need to be. We've all to bow down a bit nowadays in the House of Rimmon.[5]

Here we can see a politician privately admitting to both his contempt for ordinary people, and to the necessity, in a widening franchise, of paying public lip-service to the democratic principle. There were no doubt many real-life politicians who sympathized with this fictional one.

Words, especially perhaps political words, can be misleadingly static. Political parties retain the same name over long periods, implying sameness of identity. We habitually refer to Burke, Disraeli and Margaret Thatcher as 'Conservatives'. But the common label may conceal the differences between them. Similarly with a much older term like 'democracy'. Is there really anything in common between what was understood by the term in the time of Plato and Pericles and the meaning or meanings given to it nearly two and a half thousand years later? Or is a study of democracy bound to be a study of the diverse meanings given to a term which simply acts as a linguistic umbrella for them all?

One purpose of this book is to suggest answers to these questions. But it may be useful to give a preliminary, summary answer. So far I have stressed the flexibility and instability of the term, and the foolishness, even presumption, of attempts to fix or freeze the meanings of words of such importance. But the tendency of such an argument is in the direction of complete relativism, or an entirely arbitrary nominalism, of the type represented by Humpty Dumpty in *Through the Looking-Glass and What Alice Found There*: 'When I use a word,' Humpty Dumpty said, in rather a scornful tone, 'it means just what I choose it to mean – neither more or less.' Are we forced into that position with regard to democracy? Can it mean whatever its users choose it to mean?

At one level, the answer to this last question is yes: words themselves are not copyright. No one can prevent a word from being used in any way the user wishes, and there need be no confusion provided the user makes clear what (s)he means by the term. But the real question is, rather, whether there is any commonly accepted core of meaning among the various uses of the term which entitles us to say that this or that way of using it constitutes an abuse or misuse of it. Are all uses of meanings given to 'democracy' equally legitimate? Or do some represent a kind of verbal hijacking – an attempt to appropriate a term which does not properly or honestly belong in that context at all?

I believe that 'democracy', like 'freedom' or 'equality', is, in fact, a term with a single thread of meaning lying beneath all the varied uses and interpretations which have been made of the term. That core of meaning is necessarily general and vague enough to make such variations possible, but it is not so vague as to permit any meaning whatsoever to be placed on the word. At the root of all definitions of democracy, however refined or complex, lies the idea of popular power, of a situation in which power, and perhaps authority too, rests with the people. That power or authority is usually thought of as being political, and it often therefore takes the form of an idea of popular sovereignty – the people as the ultimate political authority. But it need not be exclusively political. Democracy is not always taken to signify only a form of government, or of choosing a government: it may be a term applied to a whole society. Alexis de Tocqueville's famous study of *Democracy in America* is primarily about American society, not its governmental or political system.

This essence or core of the conception is sufficiently basic and general to allow ample scope for the more elaborated and specific definitions we often meet. It says nothing about elections or representation. It does not indicate who comprise 'the people' – a question which, through much of its history, did not get the one answer which seems obvious and unavoidable today. It is an idea which can easily be qualified or diluted. And it can arouse

understandable hostility among those who fear 'the people' and
their aspirations. Nevertheless, it is necessarily the central element
in any plausible conception of democracy. Any claim that a certain
state or government, regime or society is 'really' or 'in the last
analysis' democratic, however implausible it may seem, must
involve the implication that in some way or other the government,
regime or state in question serves or represents the people; that the
'real' will of the people is expressed through it, or that the people
support it, even if this support is not necessarily demonstrated
through such formalities as elections. These claims may be bogus,
and very often are. They are nevertheless couched in the rhetoric
of democracy: they invoke the people and the people's will as what
legitimates the regime, or the policy or the action – which may even
be something as arbitrary as a *coup d'état*. This is the reason why
the one-party states of Communist eastern Europe styled themselves 'people's democracies'.

   That is what is distinctive about the politics of the past century,
and, to some extent, the politics of the two centuries since the
American and French revolutions. The consent, acceptance or
support of 'the people' has increasingly become the principal
source of legitimacy for governments and regimes, however
authoritarian they may be in reality. Religion, or what the Chinese
used to call 'the mandate of heaven', has not been entirely dis-
placed, and in the Islamic world has even enjoyed a revival. But
even there it is a partially democratic, popular phenomenon. Only
a religion which retains mass adherence can provide legitimacy. In
so far as Islamic laws in Iran or Pakistan, and, to a lesser extent,
Catholic laws in Ireland, command acceptance, it is because the
religion itself is popularly accepted. Where that popular base does
not exist such laws are only imposed on the population with great
difficulty, if at all.

   Even strict Muslim movements, which do not have any qualms
about imposing a rigid version of shariah law on those they govern,
whether they consent or not, are ready to use democratic arguments to boost their legitimacy. It was on the basis that they were
set to win the elections in Algeria in 1992 that the Islamic opposition there waged their cruel civil war when those elections were
abruptly cancelled.

   Invocations of popular support or consent may be baseless
and even blatantly dishonest. But 'hypocrisy is the tribute vice pays
to virtue', and in the twenty-first century democracy represents

political virtue. Those who pay lip-service to a principle they do not intend to put into practice always run the risk of being outflanked by those whose homage is more sincere. Hence the idea of democracy, or of popular power, however much and however easily it is abused and exploited, still retains a radical potential. There will always be some who are apt to ask whether existing electoral arrangements conform to the basic principle of popular power, or why this principle should not be applied in areas of privilege and power hitherto untouched by it. They are not likely to be deterred by those who contend that democracy is no more than a method of choosing national governments. Nor should they be, for if my contention is correct, they are simply discovering new applications for that basic idea of popular power; they are doing no more than engaging in the latest reinterpretation, or fresh application, of the classic democratic idea. *Eppur si muove.* Or, in this context: history moves on.

If, in briefly tracing the development of the idea of democracy from its Greek beginnings, and in exploring some of the problems which the idea of democracy involves, we hold fast to this central principle of popular power, much that might otherwise seem puzzling ought to become clear and comprehensible. That, at least, is the premise on which this book is founded.

# PART ONE
# History

# The Invention of Democracy

'Democracy', like so many central terms of politics (including 'politics'), is in origin a Greek word, combining two shorter words, *demos* and *kratos*. Both terms had more than one meaning. *Demos* could mean the whole citizen body living within a particular *polis*, or city-state, but might also be used to mean 'the mob' or 'the rabble' or 'the lower orders'. *Kratos* could mean either 'power' or 'rule': the two are not the same. It is perfectly possible to conceive of groups or individuals who have power without actually ruling in the official, visible sense. So a formal democracy, in which the people or the people's representatives appeared to rule, might conceal a very undemocratic distribution of actual power. Or conversely, a political system in which a monarch or an aristocracy formally ruled might disguise the fact that real power was in the hands of the people. This ambiguity in both constituent terms, present at the very birth of the concept and the reality of democracy, is of permanent significance in grasping its meaning and its history.

Democracy meant rule by the people or the many; but because the many were also poor, it was often taken to mean rule by the poor, or by the rabble. Aristotle is particularly clear about this. He did not think that a state in which a rich majority governed could be properly called a democracy: 'Suppose a total of one thousand three hundred; one thousand of these are rich, they give no share in government to the three hundred poor, who also are free men and in other respects like them; no one would say that these thirteen hundred lived under a democracy.' Numbers alone were not the essence of the matter. 'Whenever men rule by virtue of their wealth, be they few or many, there you have oligarchy; and where the poor rule, there you have democracy.'[1] So oligarchy meant government not simply by a few, but by a few of the 'rich and well-born'; democracy was government by the many poor.

There was a similar and complementary ambiguity about the term 'aristocracy'. Literally, this meant the rule or power of the best, but the meaning it has since acquired is not at all accidental. For it was assumed that the few who were rich and/or well-born were also, morally and politically, 'the best'. Writers such as Aristotle, and a century before him the so-called Old Oligarch – both unsympathetic to democracy – naturally used terms such as 'the virtuous', 'the noble', 'the best', 'the few', 'the notables', 'the wealthy' almost interchangeably, and contrasted this elite group with another, called variously 'the mob', 'the poor', 'the mass', 'the worse' and so on.[2]

We are not now accustomed to associate democracy with such overt expressions of class hostility and social conflict. The notion that support for democracy might mean taking sides in a kind of class war will seem absurd to most people today. Yet democracy, both in ancient Greece and in the politics of the past two centuries, has never been achieved without a struggle, and that struggle has always been, in good part, a type of class struggle, even if it is very simply characterized, as it was by many Greeks, as a struggle of the many poor against the few who are rich and well-born.

For the Greeks did not merely invent the *concept* of democracy. The concept was devised, or evolved, to describe an evolving reality – the kind of city-state in which the citizen body did actually govern itself. The *polis*, or city-state, was usually a small, self-governing, self-sustaining entity which, apart from its political autonomy, possessed very few of the characteristics of the modern state. Indeed, the term *polis* describes a certain kind of political society rather than state, if by state we mean a structure of government. Among city-states Athens was not the only democracy in the ancient Greek world but it was the most stable and long-lived, and the best documented, if only because it was politically the most important and culturally the most brilliant and creative of all the city-states. Athens will therefore serve as our model of democracy as the Greeks evolved it and understood it.

The beginning of that evolution is usually dated to the constitution which Solon produced for the city in or around 594 BC. Solon's intervention was itself the outcome of a period of conflict between 'the masses' and 'the notables', according to the account given by Aristotle in *The Athenian Constitution*.[3] Solon divided the citizen body into four classes on the basis of wealth or property ownership. While most important political offices were confined to the higher of these classes, the lowest class were entitled to attend the assembly or Ecclesia, and to make up the juries who decided both on guilt and innocence and on sentences in the courts. These were not large powers, but later changes were to enlarge them.

The next major reforms, in 508 BC, were similarly the product of conflict between the conservative aristocratic faction, led by Isagoras, and the masses, led by Cleisthenes. Isagoras invoked the aid of King Cleomenes of Sparta, and an attempt was made to restore the aristocratic oligarchy. Isagoras and the Spartans were besieged on the Acropolis by the popular forces and compelled to surrender. The way was open for radical reforms. Cleisthenes returned to Athens and instituted changes in the 'constituency' structure of the state which were designed to neutralize kinship and local allegiances and enhance the citizens' loyalty to the *polis* as a whole. The council or Boule, which met daily and prepared the agenda for meetings of the citizen assembly, was enlarged from 400 to 500 members. Each of the ten 'tribes' or constituencies chose, by lot, 50 people to serve as members of the council for a year, and those 50 would, within the council, act as a steering and administrative committee for a tenth of the year. Although the aristocratic hold on the traditional offices and institutions such as the council of the Areopagus and the office of Archon continued, power shifted to the council and the assembly.

The following fifty years, which were also the years in which Athens and the Greeks decisively rebuffed the attempts of the Persians under Darius and Xerxes to destroy their independent states, saw further moves towards the dominance of popular power in Athens, some of them directly prompted by the necessities of war. In 487 BC the archonship ceased to be an elected position, chosen by the aristocracy, and was henceforth filled by lot, while in 461 BC the council of the Areopagus, composed of the ex-archons, was deprived of its powers. From this time on the council of 500, the assembly and the popular courts, with their juries of 501, 1001, or even more – all of them filled by lot from the citizen body as a whole – became the most powerful institutions of the city-state.

So popular government was more or less firmly established from 461 BC until it was finally swept away by the Macedonian conquerors in 322 BC, to be replaced by the kind of restricted franchise which its opponents had always preferred. For democracy was never universally accepted. In fact most of the most famous Athenian philosophers and writers were critics and opponents of the democracy. Plato can reasonably be thought of as the most radically and implacably anti-democratic of all political philosophers. His mentor, Socrates, shared at least some of his views. Aristotle looked on democracy with a more tempered suspicion, but clearly viewed popular participation in politics and the popular leaders with aristocratic disdain, as did the historian Thucydides; while the comic dramatist Aristophanes mocked popular rule and its leaders time and time again, even in the years when Athens was locked in war with anti-democratic Sparta. The result is that there is no coherent and sustained statement of the classical Greek or Athenian case for democracy, while the case against it has almost monopolized the attention of posterity.

Even those who do not condemn democracy out of hand have often contrived more subtle ways of disparaging it. Thus many modern historians of classical Greece follow Thucydides and other commentators in arguing that democracy worked quite well so long as the populace was content to follow the leadership of educated spokesmen of the upper class like Pericles: 'It was he who led them, rather than they who led him ... So, in what was nominally a democracy, power was really in the hands of the first citizen ... it was under him that Athens was at her greatest.'[4] Only after Pericles' death did the rot set in, when the people insisted on following so-called 'demagogues' – revealing word – like Cleon, who evidently did not know how to behave, but curried favour with 'the rabble' by calculated populist gestures: 'He was the first', wrote Aristotle, 'to indulge in shouting and scurrilous abuse from the rostrum, and to address the people with his clothes tucked up like a common labourer, whereas all his predecessors had spoken with dignity and properly dressed.'[5] Professor Peter Green was surely right to suggest that the cult of Pericles, and the idea of a decline following his death in 429 BC, reflect the persistence of a mistrust of democracy among many modern commentators on ancient Greece.[6]

The one event that has done more than any other to damage the reputation of Athenian democracy is, of course, the trial and execution of Socrates in 399 BC for impiety and corrupting the young. Indeed, it is not too much to say that this is probably the single thing that 'everyone knows' about Athenian democracy. As

Sir Moses Finley put it: 'Here is the proof, it is said, of the tyranny of the majority . . . of the common man's hatred of the man of genius.'[7] Finley's essay in fact deals very well with both the relatively few certain facts that are known about the event and the myths that have been built up around them. The motion that Socrates was guilty was carried by 281 to 220, a close result which indicates that the decision was not the product of some universal mob hysteria. Nor can it be contended that this harsh judgement on Socrates was in any way typical of Athenian democracy's attitudes towards its critics or even its enemies. The very fact that both Plato and Aristotle spent most of their lives teaching in Athens is evidence of that. Nor can Socrates' association with some of the Thirty Tyrants who, with Spartan support, had launched a *coup* against the democracy five years earlier, have been decisive. It cannot have helped him, but the restored democracy had treated the leaders of that attempt to destroy it with, if anything, excessive leniency. Even John Stuart Mill who, as one would expect, greatly admired Socrates, describing him in *On Liberty*, rather extravagantly, as 'the head and prototype of all subsequent teachers of virtue' and 'the acknowledged master of all the eminent thinkers who have since lived', was moved to protest at this probably misplaced generosity: 'The Athenian Many, of whose irritability and suspicion we hear so much, are rather to be accused of too easy and good-natured a confidence, when we reflect that they had living in the midst of them the very men who, on the first show of an opportunity, were ready to compass the subversion of the democracy.'[8] So, while the trial and conviction of Socrates do no credit to Athenian democracy, the event's very lack of typicality ought to prevent us from drawing any grand and devastating conclusions about democracy from it. That such conclusions have nevertheless been drawn tells us more about the strength of the anti-democratic tradition in European thought than it does about Athenian democracy.

What were the central features of this democracy, which aroused such controversy at the time and still provokes debate today? The essence of it was the direct personal participation of the citizen body in the government of the city. This took two principal forms. On the one hand, there was the assembly or Ecclesia which every citizen was entitled to attend, and which took the final decisions about policy. It was the sovereign body, and it was composed of all the citizens. It met, under normal circumstances, ten times a year.

It was the concrete embodiment of the principle of popular sovereignty: not the people choosing a government once every four or five or seven years, but the people continuously governing themselves from month to month and year to year. Estimates of the size of the Athenian citizen body vary, but there were probably never more than 50,000 citizens. No doubt any one meeting was attended by half or less than half of the citizens. Yet attendance could not have been derisory, since a quorum of 6000 was needed for decisions on citizen rights and the ostracism (temporary banishment) of individuals, and such decisions were not uncommon.

The second main feature of this system of direct popular government is equally, if not more, important. It was the filling of nearly all the offices of government and administration of the laws by citizens chosen not by competitive election, but by lot. This applied to the courts, and 6000 citizens so chosen had to be available for jury service during each year. These large juries were clearly intended to provide a reasonably representative sample of popular opinion. So, of course, are juries in modern courts, but 12 people, chosen by the legal authorities and perhaps 'vetted' to eliminate 'undesirables', clearly do not constitute a microcosm of popular opinion to the same degree. Apart from the use of referenda, which are a regular feature of politics in the United States, Switzerland and some other countries, jury service, as an obligation which may in principle fall upon any citizen, is almost the sole vestige of direct citizen participation in law-making and administration which survives in modern democracies.

But in Athens it was only one of many roles which a citizen could expect to have to play in the public life of the *polis*. With the exception of the ten generals, who were elected annually by the assembly, most other public offices were filled for limited periods (usually a year) by citizens chosen by lot. This included the important Boule, or council of 500. If any body governed Athens from day to day, it was the council of 500, which met on about 300 days in the year, and which had, among other duties, the task of preparing the agenda for meetings of the assembly. But every precaution was taken to prevent it usurping the right of the people to govern themselves:

> From the fact that it was chosen by lot, with the further provision that no one might serve on it more than two years in his life, it is clear that the Athenians of the fifth and fourth centuries intended that the

council should have no chance of developing a corporate sense, which would enable it to take on an independent life, and wished it to be merely a fair sample of the Athenian people, whose views would naturally coincide with those of the people.[9]

The system of the citizens filling offices by random rotation, and of having the right to take part in the assembly, meant that Athens between, say, 462 and 322 BC came as near as any community ever has to achieving the democratic ideal of government by the people themselves, through citizen participation, rather than the modern substitutes of representation or even delegation. To ensure that participation was not, in practice, confined to those with the leisure to devote to politics, pay was introduced, first for membership of the council and for jury service, and later for attendance at the assembly. This was frequently denounced by critics of the democracy on the grounds that it introduced a pecuniary motive. But this was unfair. The pay was always very modest. What it did was to compensate working citizens for the loss of wages or earnings they would otherwise have suffered.

It was, therefore, in a sense government by amateurs; and those like Socrates and Plato, who believed that government was a specialized skill like so many other forms of specialized work, naturally viewed the Athenian experiment with anger and contempt. So did outsiders, accustomed to kingship, rule by a single person – which was, after all, to be the norm throughout the next two thousand and more years of Western history, as it was the norm in the ancient world of the Mediterranean and the Middle East. Euripides, in his play *The Suppliant Women*, sets out this antithesis in a famous dialogue between the Herald from Thebes and Theseus, the King of Athens. The Herald asks on arrival to whom he is supposed to deliver his message from King Creon: 'Who is King absolute here?' To which Theseus replies:

> This state is not
> Subject to one man's will, but is a free city.
> The king here is the people, who by yearly office
> Govern in turn. We give no special power to wealth;
> The poor man's voice commands equal authority.

The Theban Herald clearly finds this almost incomprehensible:

> The city that I come from lives under command
> Of one man, not a rabble . . .

> The common man!
> Incapable of plain reasoning, how can he guide
> A city in sound policies? Experiences gives
> More useful knowledge than impatience. Your poor rustic,
> Even though he be no fool – how can he turn his mind
> From ploughs to politics?[10]

*The Suppliant Women* was first performed in 421 BC, during the Peloponnesian War, just when Athens was forced to make a temporary peace with Sparta, and was doubtless intended to reinforce Athenian morale. But the views held by Euripides' Herald are also those of Plato's Socrates in *Protagoras*, and to some extent of the real Socrates too. Plato makes Protagoras a proponent of democracy, and Socrates is his antagonist:

> Now when we meet in the Assembly, then if the State is faced with some building project, I observe that the architects are sent for and consulted about the proposed structures, and when it is a matter of shipbuilding, the naval designers, and so on with everything which the Assembly regards as a subject for learning and teaching . . . But when it is something to do with the government of the country that is to be debated, the man who gets up to advise them may be a builder or equally well a blacksmith or a shoemaker, merchant or ship-owner, rich or poor, of good family or none. No one brings it up against any of these, . . . that here is a man who, without any technical qualifications . . . is yet trying to give advice.[11]

Protagoras' reply to this is to contend that political wisdom is not a matter of specialized knowledge, but something in which everyone has a share, and in which it is necessary that everyone has a share. 'Otherwise the state could not exist.' While not many people have adopted Plato's particular grounds for opposing democracy, the issue of expertise as opposed to supposed popular ignorance or incompetence has remained a central one in the debate about democracy.

In the modern world, democracy has often been perceived by liberals as a threat or potential threat to individual freedom, and there have been many warnings about the tyranny of the majority and the tyranny of public opinion. But in Athens freedom of speech was integral to democracy, because the process of self-government by the citizens was necessarily conducted by open debate in the assembly and in the council. Nor was there anything like modern party organization through which dissentient voices could be disciplined or silenced. Democracy and open debate were inseparable.

Similarly, it was a necessary precondition of the establishment of democracy that there should also be established the principle of equality before the law, *isonomia*. The importance of this can be seen from the fact that the Thirty Tyrants who seized power briefly in 404–3 BC decreed that only 3000 citizens should retain the right to trial, while all others could be summarily executed by government order. Popular political power was based upon the recognition of the equal status of all citizens before the law, and democracy was also the guarantee that that equality would be maintained.

It is, in fact, possible to go beyond the association of these particular principles with democracy, and say that the emergence of politics as we understand it was tied up with the emergence of democracy in ancient Greece. Politics can be quite reasonably defined as the business of government and power in any society, whatever form they may take. But both the idea of politics as a collective activity (as the business of the citizens themselves) and the idea of politics as rational, regulated government (as opposed to the arbitrary unpredictable rule of despots) pointed in the direction of democracy. 'The evolution of the Greek polis, then, is marked, above all, by an intimate connection between politicization and democratization.'[12] The idea that politics as such might have to be defended against democracy, as some contemporary writers have suggested,[13] would have been incomprehensible to the classical Athenians.

Central to the effective working of Athenian democracy was the idea of active citizenship. Citizenship did not mean mere membership in the diluted modern sense; it meant membership in its original sense, by analogy with the members or parts of the human body. It was an organic relationship which even anti-democrats like Aristotle endorsed. The state or *polis* was a whole, of which individuals were parts, dependent upon it and not self-sufficient, as the individual is often conceived to be in modern liberal thought.[14] So the citizen could only flourish as a person by acting as a part or member of the whole, the community. Pericles, in the funeral speech attributed to him by Thucydides, was clear that a withdrawal by the citizen from public life into privacy was not acceptable: 'Here each individual is interested not only in his own affairs but in the affairs of the state as well . . . we do not say that a man who takes no interest in politics is a man who minds his own business; we say that he has no business here at all.'[15] The success of the democracy depended upon the citizens' accepting their civic responsibilities, and hence upon sustaining a sense of identification with the fate of the *polis* among the citizens. 'To Pericles and his fifth-century contemporaries the private individual, or idiotes, was an idiot in our modern sense, irresponsible because unconcerned with public affairs.'[16] The Greek experience therefore raises the question whether an active, participatory democracy requires this sense of communal identity, or a collective or general interest in which individuals feel that they share, before it can function effectively.

But who comprised the citizen body? Who were 'the people'? Three major groups in Athenian society were excluded from it. First of all, it excluded without question and as a matter of course half the adult population – women. The confining of political rights, and most political activity, to men was to be characteristic of all official politics, including democratic politics, until about one hundred years ago. Second, the citizen body excluded foreigners who lived and worked in Athens, the metics. It was, in other words, a body of insiders. Third, it excluded slaves. It could only be a body of free, indigenous men. This meant that the citizens comprised a quarter or less of the total adult population. Nevertheless, as a proportion of the whole, this was far larger than any citizen body before the late eighteenth century AD.

It has often been suggested that the active self-government practised by the Athenians was only made possible by the existence of slavery, and perhaps also by the existence of empire as a source of revenue to pay for democracy. If the point of the first suggestion is that Athens was in reality the preserve of a leisured upper class, that is simply untrue. The majority of Athenian citizens were working men who needed the meagre payment that was eventually made for carrying out public duties to compensate them for the loss of daily earnings. That is why the issue of pay for office became 'a political symbol'[17] – a symbol of the determination of the democrats that poverty should not be a bar to political participation, as Pericles and Euripides boasted it was not. Whenever oligarchy took over from democracy, pay for office was one of the first things to be abolished. In Athens the political equality of the citizens co-existed uneasily with economic inequality, as it continues to do today; but the whole point of the democracy was that it gave the poor as well as the rich a part to play in governing the city. As for the second charge, that democracy, perhaps like British liberty in the nineteenth century, was parasitic upon empire, A.H.M. Jones points out that it continued to operate in the fourth century, after the loss of empire, and, indeed, was if anything more expensive then than before, since it was then that payment for attendance at the assembly was added to payment for other public duties.[18]

Many writers on democracy believe that the experience of democracy in ancient Greece has little relevance to democracy in the modern world. I have dwelt on it at some length because I believe the opposite to be the case. Most of the issues and problems involved in the definition of democracy and in the struggle to achieve it are already clear in the experience of Greek democracy. The hard struggles to realize democracy, against the entrenched interests of birth and wealth; the deprecation of democracy as the rule of 'the mob' or 'the rabble'; the conviction that the poor, or working men, have no competence in politics; the uneasy coexistence of political equality with social and economic inequality; the linking of the struggle for democracy with the struggle for freedom of speech and equality before the law; the dependence of democracy upon a communal sense of identity – all these are found in the Greek experience, and all recur in the modern evolution of democracy and the debate it generated.

Above all, it was the Greek conception of democracy which held sway until at least the time of Rousseau and *Du Contrat Social*. Democracy meant government by the people themselves; what is now tendentiously termed *direct* democracy. The election of representatives, rather than their selection by lot, was regarded by the Greeks as an aristocratic device, not a democratic one. How far direct participation on the Greek model is possible in the modern world is, of course, another matter; although a citizen body of 40,000 is a great deal larger than many present-day groups or institutions which would regard direct democracy as impracticable, as well as undesirable. The result of this direct participation of the citizens was something very remarkable, something almost undreamt of in the modern world: 'There was scarcely any separate or professional state apparatus in the city, . . . Athenian democracy signified, precisely, the refusal of any division between "state" and "society".'[19] It will do no harm to recall that that is what democracy originally meant and in fact was: state and society at one, the citizen body governing itself directly, through active participation in politics, a duty which fell upon every citizen at one time or another.

# The Re-emergence of Democracy

Probably the basic ideas of democracy – the idea of equal political rights for all (or at least for all men), the idea of a government of the poor or of the people, the idea of turning the traditional social hierarchies upside down – have never entirely disappeared among the vast submerged majorities in history. Certainly such aspirations surface with extraordinary promptness at moments of crisis or revolution. 'When Adam delved, and Eve span,/Who was then the gentleman?' asked the English protesters of 1381. Some of those who took part in Ket's Rebellion in Norfolk in 1549 were reported as saying that 'gentlemen have ruled aforetime, and they (the commons, that is) will rule now'.[1] The task of uncovering, or recovering, the ideas and aspirations of these hidden majorities has been started, but remains perhaps the central project for historians in a democratic age. It is still little more than a century since the Putney debates of 1647 were first published and the significance of the Levellers began to be appreciated. The Diggers are an even more recent discovery. The history of women and women's movements is still being written, and there is much still to be discovered.

It is therefore impossible to be dogmatic about the precise beginnings of modern democratic thinking and politics. But the complexity of democracy's evolution derives from at least two major streams. On the one hand, there is the egalitarianism inherent in Reformation Protestantism, as well as the theory and practice of resistance to established rulers, and even of radical democracy, which evolved out of it. On the other hand, there is the ideological and institutional inheritance of feudalism: the assemblies of privileged estates, usually aristocracy, clergy and commons, which had developed within feudal societies and were intended to be roughly representative of wider social constituencies or groupings. That these two streams should eventually have converged may have the appearance of inevitability in retrospect. But there was nothing predictable or harmonious about it.

It was certainly no part of the intentions of the founders of Protestantism to encourage discontent or disobedience. Luther held that it was 'better to obey a prince doing wrong than a people doing right', and he drew a sharp distinction between things spiritual and things temporal; between the rules and values appropriate to the inner life of the soul and those appropriate to life in the fallen and sinful external world. 'The gospel does not become involved in the affairs of this world', he told the protesting peasants of Swabia in 1525. The distinction between the two kingdoms, of God and of this world, though fundamental, was a difficult one to draw. Both Luther and Calvin accepted that secular rulers had no jurisdiction over spiritual matters. But who was to judge where the spiritual ended and the secular began? The egalitarian doctrine of the priesthood of all believers was intended to apply only to matters spiritual; but it was Luther who pointed out, 'When a priest is murdered the whole country is placed under interdict', and asked, 'Why not when a peasant is murdered?'[2] It was hardly surprising that many of the humbler converts to Protestantism should interpret this doctrine as egalitarian in a wider social and political sense. The Elizabethan nobleman who defended the episcopate because 'As they shoot at bishops now, so will they do at the nobility also, if they be suffered',[3] was not wide of his mark.

The belief that God spoke directly to individuals gave Protestants a confidence in themselves and a dedication to their cause which ordinary people in the West had probably never known before. From this religious dedication, which was not exclusive to Protestants, sprang the modern era's first experiments in popular power. To call them 'democracies' might arouse the wrong expectations. They were not open or tolerant, and their popular character ensured that they were viewed with fear and horror by the propertied classes. The so-called Anabaptists' take-over of Münster in 1536 became for more than a century afterwards a byword among the respectable for the supposed anarchy, savagery and madness which were bound to result if ever the 'multitude' gained political power. Calvinist Ghent in the 1570s and Paris under the domination of the Catholic League were perhaps the first sustained exercises in popular power in the modern period, and even they did not last long.

Just as important was the way in which, after the horrific Massacre of St Bartholomew in Paris in 1572, the French Huguenots were driven to formulate a theory to justify their resistance to a Catholic ruler, a theory which was then taken up by the Dutch in their epoch-making resistance to Spanish rule in the Netherlands. The theory of resistance had its roots in the traditional distinction between a king and a tyrant, and the consequent argument that while lawful kings should not be resisted, it could be a duty to oppose a tyrant. In the political literature of Calvinism in the 1570s this old argument is pushed significantly further.

For François Hotman, the author of *Francogallia*, as well as for the (still uncertain) author of the *Vindiciae contra Tyrannos* (1579), and for the Scottish writer George Buchanan, whose tract *De Jure Regni apud Scotos* appeared in the same year as the *Vindiciae*, it is for the people to decide when and if a ruler has become a tyrant. For all three authors the ultimate source of royal authority is not God, or tradition, but the people, whether through some original popular decision to set up a monarchy, or through a constantly renewed popular choice of rulers. Hotman points out that while 'there may be a people without a king ... a king without a people is as inconceivable as a pastor without a flock',[4] and suggests that the supposed ancient kingdom of Francogallia 'was not subject to the law of inheritance as if it were a private patrimony but was habitually transferred by the votes and decisions of the people' (p. 247). Hotman invoked a conjectural past to challenge the hereditary principle and assert the right of the people to choose their rulers, even though the issue of tyranny might not arise. The author of the *Vindiciae* similarly asserts that since 'none were ever born with crowns on their heads and sceptres in their hands, and [since] no man can be a king by himself, nor reign without a people ... it must of necessity follow, that kings were at first constituted by the people.' He adds, meaningfully: 'In all well-ordered kingdoms, this custom is yet remaining.'[5] George Buchanan also contends that it is the people who are the ultimate source of the laws: 'the Law is more powerful than the King, and the People more powerful than the Law' for 'the People is as it were the Parent of the Law, certainly the Author thereof'.[6] Buchanan also argues, as does the *Vindiciae*, that the function of a monarchy is to serve the good of the people, and this was echoed in the Dutch Edict of Renunciation of

1581: 'the subjects are not created by God for the benefit of the Prince ... On the contrary, the Prince is created for the subjects.'[7]

Here, then, at the opening of the modern era, we have a quite well-developed doctrine of popular sovereignty. The people make the laws and select their rulers. Their rulers are also their servants. These were radical claims to make, not least because there was developing at exactly the same time a theory of absolute, unlimited sovereignty which became the intellectual basis for the absolutism which was the dominant pattern of rule in Europe in the seventeenth and eighteenth centuries. In some countries, such as Russia and Austria, absolutism even lasted into the twentieth century. The principal contemporary exponent of this theory was Jean Bodin, whose *Les Six Livres de la République* also appeared in the 1570s. For him:

> The principal mark of sovereign majesty and absolute power is essentially the right to impose laws on subjects generally without their consent ... Law is nothing other than the command of the sovereign in the exercise of his power.[8]

As absolutism took hold in the seventeenth century, many traditional assemblies of estates fell into abeyance, and, contrary to the popular mythology of peaceful evolution of modern institutions, the gradual evolution of such an assembly into a modern parliament, as took place in England, was the exception rather than the rule in early modern Europe.

But who constituted 'the people', whose rights against monarchs were so ringingly asserted by the Calvinist and Huguenot writers? Here we encounter that fear of the many, the multitude, which is to be a recurring motif in the re-emergence of democracy in the modern era. Both Buchanan and the author of the *Vindiciae* deal explicitly with the charge that they are placing ultimate political power in the hands of the multitude, 'the beast with many heads', as both authors refer to it. In the *Vindiciae* the reply is that 'when we speak of all the people, we understand by that, only those who hold their authority from the people, to wit, the magistrates ... whom the people have substituted, or established ... to represent the whole body of the people. We understand also, the assembly of the estates ...' (p. 97). Buchanan took a similar if slightly more radical line. Hotman's case is particularly interesting in that where in the first version the word *populus* was used, in the 1576 edition the term *ordines*, meaning orders of estates, was inserted to 'clarify' the meaning, or, we might suspect, to reassure those alarmed by the dangerously democratic sound of the first version.

These writers were faced with a fundamental tactical problem in the development of democratic theory. It was clear that some notion of popular sovereignty provided the only plausible basis on which to challenge the theory and practice of absolutism. But the language of popular sovereignty is by its nature universalist. How was such a language to be used, in the interests of the responsible and respectable, without placing an ideological weapon in the hands of 'the multitude' and of those who claimed to speak on its behalf? The problem was how to exploit the power of appeals to 'the people' while at the same time defining 'the people' in ways narrow enough to exclude the majority of actual persons, both male and female. It is a dilemma that recurs throughout the history of liberal and democratic movements, as radical groups repeatedly push the logic of an apparently universal claim further than the respectable classes ever intended.

Among such groups were the Levellers, who emerged as a significant political force in England in the late 1640s. They have a good claim to be considered 'the world's first organized radical-democratic political party'. For, as A.L. Morton pointed out, they had a published programme of comprehensive reforms and policies. They had a leadership, and members who paid dues and were organized in local groups.[9] They were not, however, a Parliamentary party. They had some support in Parliament, but their strength lay outside it, and their strategy was to mobilize this support, through demonstrations, petitions, and by organizing within the army. Parliament, elected before the civil war, was no longer representative of opinion among those who had fought against the King. As it has often done in the modern period, the experience of war had given those who had taken part in it and survived it a new and more confident awareness of their own worth and standing. The Levellers articulated this awareness, and channelled it into a coherent set of democratic political demands. In the famous debates between the Levellers and the army leaders, principally Cromwell and Ireton, at Putney in the autumn of 1647, the Levellers argued that those who had fought on Parliament's side had earned the right to be enfranchised: 'if ever a people shall free themselves from tyranny, certainly it is after seven years' war and fighting for their liberty',[10] said Maximilian Petty. And when Ireton argued that the franchise should be restricted to property holders, Edward Sexby retorted angrily:

> There are many thousands of us soldiers that have ventured our lives;
> we have had little propriety [i.e. property] in the kingdom as to our
> estates, yet we have had a birthright. But it seems now, except a man
> hath a fixed estate in this kingdom, he hath no right in this kingdom.
> I wonder we were so much deceived. If we had not a right to the
> kingdom, we were mere mercenary soldiers. (p. 69)

When Ireton enquired whether the proposed new constitution, the
*Agreement of the People*, implied that every male inhabitant should
have a vote, Colonel Thomas Rainborough answered with a now
famous statement of the principle of government by popular
consent:

> For really I think that the poorest he that is in England hath a life to
> live, as the greatest he; and therefore truly, sir, I think it's clear, that
> every man that is to live under a government ought first by his own
> consent to put himself under that government; and I do think that the
> poorest man in England is not at all bound in a strict sense to that
> government that he hath not had a voice to put himself under; . . .
> (p. 53)

John Wildman said much the same: 'I conceive that's the undeni-
able maxim of government: that all government is in the free consent of the people' (p. 66).

But even with the Levellers we have to ask: who count as the
people? Clearly not women – although women Levellers on at least
one occasion asserted 'an equal interest with the men of this nation
in those liberties and securities contained in the Petition of Right,
and other the good laws of the land' (p. 367). It has been argued by
C.B. Macpherson that the Levellers also wanted to exclude all
wage-earners, or employees, from the franchise. This, I believe,
does less than justice to their egalitarianism.[11] But it does seem
clear that at various times the Levellers did allow that in practice
not all men would be enfranchised by their proposals. Once again
a universalist rhetoric disguises a rather more restricted reality.

Nevertheless the Levellers did challenge the traditional view that
political rights belonged exclusively to property- or landowners,
and asserted the democratic proposition that those persons whom
Cromwell loftily described as having 'no interest but the interest
of breathing' had political rights too. They also asserted the
supremacy of the people over Parliament. Thus the author of *A
Remonstrance of Many Thousand Citizens*, probably Richard
Overton, reminded the House of Commons in 1646 that 'wee are

your Principalls, and you our Agents; . . . wee possessed you with
the same Power that was in our selves . . . For wee might justly
have done it our selves without you, if we had thought it
convenient; . . .'.[12]

We should note that we have already moved some way from the
Greek conception of democracy as government by the people
themselves. The issue is the people's right to choose their representatives and to hold them accountable; and, in this English
context, Parliament has already become the focus of the struggle
for democracy, as it was to remain in subsequent centuries. On the
other hand, the Levellers never accepted that sovereignty resided
in Parliament. The people, however defined, were sovereign, and
Members of Parliament were their agents, there to execute the
popular will. Those MPs who failed to do so should be replaced.
The Levellers favoured annual, or at least biennial, elections, and
suggested that no one should be allowed to stand as a candidate for
two successive parliaments. They also wished to see the principle
of popular election extended beyond Parliament, and suggested
that magistrates and judges should be elected annually.[13] Popular
power was at the heart of their vision of a new political and social
order.

But it was the more conservative views of Cromwell and Ireton
that prevailed in practice. Property remained the precondition of
political rights, and Ireton's argument at Putney that 'liberty cannot
be provided for in a general sense, if property [is to] be preserved'
(p. 73) was accepted by the ruling property-owners as a necessary
truth of politics. Particularly after the political settlement of 1688–9,
it was ever more openly asserted that political power belonged, as
of right, to the propertied.

The philosopher whose name is always associated with the
1688–9 settlement in England is, of course, John Locke, even
though his *Second Treatise of Government*, which was taken as an
apologia for that settlement, was most probably written as a
response to the Exclusion crisis of 1679–80. Locke is rightly
identified with the development of liberal political thought, and so,
by a common mode of thinking, his name is also linked to the idea
of democracy. What is the justification for this? For Locke, civil
government, as opposed to tyranny or despotism, must be founded
on contract and consent. Government is a trust held on behalf of
the people. If that trust is breached, as the Whigs held that it had
been by James II, the people have the right to resist the government

and replace it with another. Locke thus belongs to the tradition of contract theory which usually carries with it an implication of ultimate political power and rights belonging to the people; and the fact that he explicitly develops and allows for a right of resistance also gave his doctrine a subversive potential of which later radicals made effective use.

On the other hand, Locke's notion of government by consent is not democracy. The people can consent to whatever form of civil or constitutional rule they like. 'Locke is attempting to establish the proper source of authority for any government. Locke does not distinguish between forms of government on the basis of consent.'[14] It is to a system or structure of government that consent is required, not to particular governments, let alone particular decisions or policies.

What is more, Locke's interpretation of what consent involves is so accommodating as to evacuate the notion of much substance. Since only adults can give consent, he is bound logically to admit that a child 'is born a Subject of no Country or Government'.[15] A (male) adult gives his consent when he comes of age. How? By accepting whatever property he may inherit from his father. But what about those who have nothing to inherit? About them Locke is silent. Is it really the case that consent is not required from non-property-owners? Locke's defenders are unwilling to admit that this might be so. On the other hand, it seems implausible that most male English adults readily consented to having no political rights, as would seem to be the implication of Locke's arguing that England was a country with government by consent. Locke also suggests that a man's presence in a particular state implies tacit consent to its political system. In this way the apparently active and positive concept of consent is diluted to the point of near vacuity.

The notorious ambiguity of Locke's conception of property, which at times means 'Lives, Liberties and Estates', and at others only 'Estates' or property in the ordinary sense, also makes it unclear whether government exists for the benefit of all, or only for property-owners in the usual sense. That society should have a two-tier membership, with only property-owners possessing full political rights, as C.B. Macpherson has suggested,[16] may or may not have been what Locke believed. But it certainly suited the dominant landed gentry to interpret him in that way. Thus the principles of popular sovereignty, consent and the right of resistance, with all their potentially radical implications, were absorbed by Locke into a theory which had property and property rights at its core. Potentially democratic ideas thus provided a justification for rule by a propertied oligarchy. As Basil Willey put it: 'The "Rights of Man" as yet are the rights of proprietors'.[17]

Meanwhile 'the multitude' or 'the mob' – the latter term came into common use at this period – were explicitly excluded from orthodox definitions of 'the people'. Locke's friend, James Tyrrell, spelt this out: 'I desire the reader to remember that I do not make use of the word people for the mere vulgar or mobile, but for the whole community, consisting of clergy, nobility and commons'; and 'when I make use of the word people, I do not mean the vulgar or mixed multitude'.[18] Similarly, the term 'freemen', also current, was used in a very restricted way, as when Lord Hardwicke declared in 1757, 'Our men of property are our only freemen'.[19] Daniel Defoe distinguished between freeholders and mere inhabitants, and argued that since freeholders owned the country, they had the right to make the laws and impose them upon the inhabitants, who were only in effect 'lodgers', as he put it.[20] It was argued that only property-owners had the economic independence necessary to be free men. One deduction from this could have been that property should be as widely dispersed as possible, to enlarge the bounds of the citizen body. But after 1688, Parliament under Whig domination tended to restrict rather than enlarge the franchise, and some people even lost their voting rights. The length of each parliament was extended from three to seven years by an act of 1716, and many elections were uncontested.[21] The eighteenth century was not a period of gradual progress towards democracy in Britain, as Whig historians have tried to suggest, but of a determined retreat from it. The poor, or 'the mob or mere dregs of the people' as Henry Fox, father of Charles James, once called them, were seen not only as wholly unfit to rule, being ignorant and lacking the independence which property supposedly conferred, but even as a threat to the freedom for which England was internationally renowned. 'The greater the share the people have in government,' said John Wesley, 'the less liberty, civil or religious, does a nation enjoy.'[22]

Edmund Burke, the Whig politician who became the founding philosopher of modern British Conservatism, would certainly have agreed with that. Burke's name is often associated not just with Conservatism but with the underlying philosophy of British democratic politics as a whole, principally on account of his observations on the role of party in politics, and on the nature of representation (the latter being discussed below, in Chapter 8). This is revealing in its way, for Burke was certainly no democrat. Reacting against the enthusiasm with which so many people, including Whig friends and colleagues like Charles James Fox, greeted the outbreak of the French Revolution, Burke denounced democracy in vehement terms. He was contemptuous of the idea that one person's vote should count equally with any other's: 'It is said, that twenty-four millions ought to prevail over two hundred thousand. True; if the constitution of a kingdom be a problem of arithmetic.' He was also one prime source of the notion that has counted for so much among those with misgivings about democracy ever since: that of the tyranny of the majority. 'The tyranny of the multitude is but a multiplied tyranny.'[23]

Of course it is quite true that Burke was a firm believer in parliamentary government and parliamentary sovereignty; but that is not the same thing. The parliament he defended, and whose reform he opposed, was one dominated by large landowners. In Burke's view, which was orthodox in his time, this was entirely as it should be. Landowners ought to rule. Certainly ability as well as property ought to find a place in the legislature, but property ought to be 'out of all proportion, predominant in the representation'. And it was right, too, that the big property-owners should dominate: 'they form a natural rampart about the lesser properties in all their gradations' (p. 140). Burke estimated that 'the people', by which he meant those who ought to enjoy voting rights, comprised about 400,000 people in England and Scotland. So far from allowing that that number might increase, in 1769 he even favoured a reduction of the number of the enfranchised.[24]

The French Revolution, by espousing an equality which suggested that 'all occupations were honourable', and that such menial persons as 'hairdressers' and 'tallow-chandlers' were entitled to a say in politics, was setting itself at war with the natural order of human society, in Burke's view:

> Such descriptions of men ought not to suffer oppression from the state; but the state suffers oppression, if such as they, either individually or collectively, are permitted to rule. In this you think you are combatting prejudice, but you are at war with nature. (p. 138)

Even the liberal-minded luminaries of the French Enlightenment, for all their courageous championship of tolerance and freedom of opinion, were by no means democrats. Diderot believed that political rights belonged to property-owners, and Voltaire similarly identified 'the people' with the middle class. The notoriously atheist and materialist Holbach was explicit about whom he meant by 'the people':

> By the word people I do not mean the stupid populace ... Every man who can live respectably from the income of his property and every head of a family who owns land ought to be regarded as a citizen.

Others could not become citizens 'until by their labour and industry they have acquired land'.[25] It is the Whig view in essence. It is still land which confers the privilege of citizenship.

But while the poor, the mob, the dregs were to be firmly excluded from political life, the developing study of political economy recognized that these same ignorant and brutal multitudes played an indispensable economic role. Thus Dean Hickes wrote, as early as 1684: 'the poor are the hands and feet of the body politic ... They plough our land and dig our quarries and cleanse our streets ... No commonweal can subsist without poor.'[26] Or, as Bernard Mandeville put it, in his usual ambivalent, ironic manner: 'it is manifest, that in a Free Nation, where Slaves are not allowed of, the surest wealth consists in a multitude of laborious poor'.[27] Thus a Free Nation coexisted with the mass of the unfranchised poor. The poor were economically necessary but politically threatening. Here was a condition of contradiction which could not last for ever.

# Popular Politics

It was not until the French Revolution that *democracy* ceased to be a
mere literary word, and became part of the political vocabulary.

Ernest Weekley[1]

It was not primarily *ideas* of democracy, which, as we have seen,
only enjoyed a diluted existence in the eighteenth century, but
popular action, and above all the eruption of the French people into
politics in the years of the Revolution, that transformed the modern
history of democracy. At a stroke, we might almost say, political
ideas which had only been aspirations or dreams in the minds of
philosophers or popular radicals, were placed on the agenda of real
politics, not only in France or even Europe, but globally. The
principles and example of the Revolution helped to inspire the first
successful slave revolt in the Caribbean in Haiti, as well as the
political independence movements of South America. All such
movements raised the issue of democracy, of popular power.

They raised the issue, but they did not necessarily resolve it. For
the old fear of the mob was intensified by the now much greater
possibility of the people obtaining real political power and political
rights. It is therefore in the age of modern popular politics after
1789, the age of movement towards democracy, that we see also the
development of an opposition to democracy with a more sophisticated theoretical basis than any since the time of Plato.

This opposition and critique is first articulated in the American
debates surrounding the Declaration of Independence in 1776 and
the writing of a constitution a decade later. With the future of a new
state lying uncharted before them, discussion of politics naturally
reached down to basic principles. There was considerable pressure

to establish the new states and their federation as democracies, or as near that as was practically possible, democracy still at this time meaning direct popular participation in government. There was discussion of the rotation of offices, and there were demands for annual elections. Thomas Paine was one radical who accepted the inevitability of representative rather than direct democracy, but urged that in order 'that the *elected* might never form to themselves an interest separate from the electors, *prudence* will point out the propriety of having elections often'.[2] In New York such menial types as 'carpenters, cobblers and butchers' demanded that the state constitution should be subject to ratification by popular referendum. In Massachusetts, William Gordon objected to the idea of confining political rights to the propertied: 'The rich will have enough advantage against the poor without political advantage. Mere riches are no qualification. Why should the want of them be a disqualification?'[3] The democrats generally favoured single-chamber or unicameral legislatures as the most direct way of reflecting or embodying the popular will.

For the most part, however, it was not the democrats who carried the day, but the Whig Founding Fathers, who were as concerned as their British counterparts to establish restraints on the popular will, to protect the interests of the rich and propertied, and to restrict the franchise to property-holders. It was true, of course, that property was dispersed much more widely than in Europe. Thus the property qualification for voting in Maryland, although higher than many people wanted, nevertheless enfranchised more than half the free male population.[4] Jefferson, a comparative radical among the constitution makers, proposed, for his own state of Virginia, measures to distribute land more widely in order to enfranchise as many as possible of the male and free population. He mistrusted the rich, and frequently proclaimed his faith in the people. But like so many of his contemporaries, he had a selective vision of who 'the people' were which did not prevent him from referring on occasion, like Burke, to the 'swinish multitude'.[5]

Jefferson criticized the Virginia constitution for being too unified, with all the power concentrated in the legislature. This, he maintained, could lead to despotism:

> 173 despots would surely be as oppressive as one ... An *elective despotism* was not the government we fought for; but one ... in which the powers of government should be so divided and balanced among

several bodies or magistracies, as that no one could transcend their legal limits, without being effectually checked and restrained by the others.'[6]

What he and his colleagues were aiming at was not democracy, popular government, but limited government, or what they termed a 'republic' or a 'representative republic'. In it the poor would have a voice and a share, but would not be able to outweigh or vote away the interests of the propertied and the wealthy. 'All communities divide themselves into the few and the many. The first are the rich and well-born, the other the mass of the people', Hamilton was reported as saying at the Federal Convention in 1787. 'Give all power to the many, they will oppress the few. Give all power to the few, they will oppress the many.' Hence there was a need to give 'the rich and well-born' a 'distinct, permanent share in the government' through which they could 'check the imprudence of democracy'.[7] It might have been Aristotle speaking. This checking role was to be played by the Senate, as John Adams explained:

> The rich ought to have an effectual barrier in the constitution against being robbed, plundered, and murdered, as well as the poor; and this can never be without an independent Senate.[8]

On the whole, the makers of the American federal and state constitutions were well satisfied with their work. Power was indeed divided, in such a way as to place restraints upon popularly elected assemblies; and it was the view of Hamilton that a representative democracy avoided the dangers clearly inherent in 'simple democracy':

> When the deliberative or judicial powers are vested wholly or partly in the collective body of the people, you must expect error, confusion and instability. But a representative democracy, where the right of election is well secured and regulated, and the exercise of the legislative, executive and judiciary authorities is vested in selected persons chosen really and not nominally by the people, will in my opinion be most likely to be happy, regular and durable.[9]

The intention was that the electors should choose to be governed by persons they recognized as better and wiser than themselves, who might well understand better than the people themselves what their real interests were, and whose decisions the people would therefore accept.[10] John Stuart Mill later expressed much the same view. A representative system of government, coupled with a division of powers, was thus seen as providing safeguards against the dangers of democracy.

Paradoxically enough, we can perceive here the germ of an alternative version of democracy to the idea of popular rule. This is rooted in the perception of society as a collection of disparate and even conflicting interests – such as those of the rich and poor – with a democratic system of government being one in which these different interests are recognized as legitimate and therefore have a voice. 'Those who hold, and those who are without property, have ever formed distinct interests in society.'[11] Class and inequality are accepted as permanent and ineradicable, and are embodied in an uneasy equilibrium within the political system itself. We can see here the beginnings of modern pluralist theory.

In France, however, quite a different tradition of thinking about democracy was developing. This saw the common interest as something other than the sum of, or compromise between, a diversity of group interests. It was, indeed, antithetical to sectional interests. The prime source of this tradition of thought was Jean-Jacques Rousseau. Rousseau's conception of society, at least in *Du Contrat Social*, was the exact opposite of that of individualist writers like Hobbes and Bentham, for whom society was in essence a collection of discrete individuals, held together by laws and authority. Rousseau was emphatic that the general interest of society was not the mere sum of individuals' interests, any more than the general will was the mere sum of individual wills. He was therefore equally clear that majority decisions would not necessarily embody the general will or express the general interest. That would depend on whether each person acted or voted solely in his or her own interest, or considered the good of the community and acted accordingly. In this at least he agreed with Madison and the other American constitutionalists, who also did not believe that majority decisions were necessarily right. But whereas they concluded from this that it was desirable to devise institutional checks on the will of the majority, Rousseau accepted the principle of majority decisions but tried to envisage conditions under which the majority would truly represent the community as a whole and not simply a collection of group or individual interests.

His conclusions in this respect were generally pessimistic and nostalgic. Only in small and relatively unified societies, not fragmented by industrialization and the resultant division of labour, was it likely that citizens would be more aware of their membership of society as a whole than of their particular social, occupational or interest group within it. This, however, did not prevent him from becoming a cult figure among some of the Jacobins and other revolutionaries. Whether correctly or not, he was interpreted as the philosopher of the sovereignty of the popular or general will over all partial or sectional interests. To the American Founding Fathers and Whigs like Burke such a notion pointed towards a democratic or popular tyranny, and threatened the rights of minorities and individuals. But many democrats, in France and elsewhere, were determined that the traditionally dominant minority of the rich and propertied should no longer be able to stand in the way of the will and the interests of the great majority.

In his famous pamphlet of 1789, *What is the Third Estate?*,[12] the Abbé Sieyès proclaimed that the third estate, the commons, was not one order alongside the two others, the nobility and clergy, but was the nation itself. The old orders had no place, since the nation was a single entity with a single will (pp. 154ff.). But as to who comprised the nation, or the people, the Abbé was clear that it did not include everyone:

> Thus, rightly or wrongly, women are everywhere excluded from mandates of this kind. It is unquestionable that tramps or beggars cannot be charged with the political confidence of nations. Would a servant, or any person under the domination of a master, or a non-naturalized foreigner, be permitted to appear among the representatives of a nation? Political liberty, therefore, has its limits . . . (pp. 74–5)

He was also for excluding the old privileged orders from the newly enfranchised nation.

The issue of the franchise did not, however, make up the sum total of what was generally understood by democracy at that revolutionary moment. When Wordsworth confessed in a letter of 1794 that 'I am of that odious class of men called democrats', he was indicating that he was not so much a supporter of a wider parliamentary franchise as on the side of the people, and that he was a social and political egalitarian, though not necessarily also an economic one: 'my heart was all/Given to the people, and my love was theirs', recalled the poet in *The Prelude* (1805, Book IX, 124–5). Democracy signified a particular type of society, and not merely a particular form of government, or of choosing a government. Wordsworth regarded the Cumberland of his childhood as possessing some of the Rousseauesque characteristics of such a society:

> ... born in a poor district ...
> It was my fortune scarcely to have seen
> Through the whole tenor of my school-day time
> The face of one, who, whether boy or man,
> Was vested with attention or respect
> Through claims of wealth or blood; ...

while at Cambridge University he found

> That something there was holden up to view
> Of a Republic, where all stood thus far
> Upon equal ground; that they were brothers all
> In Honour, as of one community, ...

> (IX, 217, 221–5, 228–31)

A recognition of the worth of every human being, however obscure or impoverished, and a new stress on the positive virtues of the working poor, as well as their contribution to social and economic life – these were some aspects of the democratic spirit of the times, expressed by Wordsworth in many of his poems about the people of his native region, such as 'Resolution and Independence', 'Michael', and 'The Old Cumberland Beggar'. It is in this faith in 'ordinary' people, whose qualities were far from ordinary in Wordsworth's eyes, that we find the justification for political demands for popular power or a wider franchise.

Another Romantic poet, Byron, challenged the conventional view of popular protest as the actions of 'the mob' when he defended the Luddites in his maiden speech in the House of Lords in 1812:

> You call these men a mob, desperate, dangerous, and ignorant ... Are we aware of our obligations to a mob? It is the mob that labour in your fields and serve in your houses, – that man your navy and recruit your army ... You may call the people a mob; but do not forget that a mob too often speaks the sentiments of the people.[13]

True, Byron on another occasion defined democracy as 'an Aristocracy of Blackguards' (p. 434), and mistrusted popular leaders and advocates like Paine and Cobbett. Nevertheless, as between the old order and 'the peoples', he sided in sentiment and active commitment with the latter:

> The king-times are fast finishing. There will be blood shed like water, and tears like mist; but the peoples will conquer in the end. I shall not live to see it, but I foresee it. (p. 372)

This broad and deep conception of democracy explains why Tocqueville's *Democracy in America* is a study of American society, more concerned with social and economic equality and their political implications than with democracy narrowly conceived of as a purely political system. In 1836, the year that Tocqueville's book appeared, his admirer John Stuart Mill wrote that 'High wages and universal reading are the two elements of democracy; where they co-exist, all government, except the government of public opinion, is impossible'.[14] Whole societies were being democratized, and it was often the case that the extension of the franchise followed upon this process and reflected it, rather than being the sole or dominant issue in the nineteenth-century debate on democracy. Thus, on the eve of the second British Reform Act of 1867, James Bryce noted that 'the social progress of democracy has outrun its political progress', which was ominous because 'there is nothing more dangerous than a democratic society without democratic institutions'.[15] A democratic society was one in which the mass of the people played an active rather than a passive role, and in which the old traditions of deference and subordination had been replaced by a sense of equality among the people – the feeling that one man, or even one person, is as good as another, or at least has an equal right to be respected and listened to. Thus there is inevitably a link between democracy and equality. Only when enough people possess a strong sense of their own worth and rights can the demand for a popular franchise, or equal political rights, be made to any effect.

One very influential form of the belief in the equal rights or worth of each person was found in Utilitarianism, which in its democratic version attached equal weight to the happiness and suffering of each individual. It was not simply the lump sum of human happiness which had to be increased, but also its even distribution throughout the population. But how was this to be achieved? Until the American and French Revolutions Bentham and other Utilitarians hoped that they could persuade apparently enlightened rulers or despots to commit themselves to the self-evidently admirable aim of increasing the sum and the spread of human well-being. This hope was disappointed. After 1789, Bentham, who was among that distinguished band of foreigners on whom the Revolution conferred honorary French citizenship, saw that the people were capable of acting politically for themselves, and was converted to the general principle of political democracy.[16] Since each person pursued his or her own well-being, it followed that each person would vote in his or her own interest. The sum total of individual votes ought therefore to promote the Utilitarian objective of the greatest happiness of the greatest number. The only people who could be trusted to pursue the good of the people were the people themselves, acting through their elected and accountable representatives: 'as to universal suffrage,' wrote Bentham in 1817, 'what principle could be more impregnable?'.[17]

This argument was set out with particular clarity by James Mill in his celebrated *Essay on Government*, first published in 1820. Having shown, as he believed, that monarchies and aristocracies would inevitably pursue their own good at the expense of the general good, Mill is compelled to recognize that only the community as a whole can be trusted to pursue the general good. But it is equally clear that direct, participatory democracy is, if not impossible, at least not very practicable in the modern world, and is in any case a recipe for bad government: 'a community in mass is ill adapted for the business of Government ... all numerous assemblies are essentially incapable of business'.[18] The way out of this dilemma is found through the device of representation: 'In the grand discovery of modern times, the system of representation, the solution of all the difficulties, both speculative and practical, will perhaps be found' (p. 73). The sanction of frequent elections is the check which the people have over their representatives, while the representatives themselves must have the power to check the executive. In these ways Mill believed that the interests of the governors and the governed could be brought into accord.

The argument that the principle of democracy could be reconciled with the fact of size through the device of representation was not original to Mill. One of the first to make the case had been Tom Paine in *Rights of Man* (1791–2):

> Referring, then, to the original simple democracy, it affords the true data from which governments on a large scale can begin. It is incapable of extension, not from its principle, but from the inconvenience of its form ... Simple democracy was society governing itself without the aid of secondary means. By ingrafting representation upon democracy, we arrive at a system of government capable of embracing and confederating all the various interests and every extent of territory and population ...[19]

Mill, unlike Paine, felt obliged, however, to meet the common bourgeois objection against universal male suffrage that the mass of the people were not fit to govern, and would use political power to 'plunder the rich', as Macaulay charged in his formidable attack on Mill's *Essay*. Mill's reply, in effect, was that the middle class, 'the class which is universally described as both the most wise and the most virtuous part of the community', would still dominate in a democracy, because, 'Of the people beneath them, a vast majority would be sure to be guided by their advice and example' (pp. 93–4). Middle-class radical reformers stuck to this sanguine view. Edward Miall argued in the 1840s that enfranchising the working class would give them that sense of citizen responsibility which they were said to lack, and that as a result the middle class would be able to 'lead them almost whithersoever they please'.[20] Although Macaulay ridiculed Mill's expectation, it turned out to be remarkably accurate. Universal franchise has not produced the working-class political dominance which so many people in the nineteenth century on both sides of the debate either feared or hoped it would.

Paine, Bentham and, to a lesser degree, James Mill shared in the optimistic mood of the decades after 1789, when it was possible for a radical like William Hazlitt to affirm, without qualification or self-consciousness, that '*Vox populi vox Dei*, is the rule of all good Government'. It was the historic moment when the rule of the people, the idea of democracy, was seen as the only legitimate form of government and as the key to sweeping away the rule of individual despots and arrogant oligarchies, and when articulate voices were not afraid to proclaim their faith in the virtues and good judgement of the people as a whole.

But by 1820 the moment was already passing. And the anointed heir of the British Utilitarian tradition, James Mill's son, John Stuart, soon moved away from the robust democratic faith of his early mentors. Under the influence of a variety of thinkers, including Thomas Carlyle, Saint-Simon and Tocqueville, the younger Mill came to share and articulate the doubts felt about democracy by so many nineteenth-century liberals. Quite early on 'I ceased to consider representative democracy as an absolute principle', he wrote later, 'and regarded it as a question of time, place, and circumstance'.[21] And of his views in the 1840s he wrote: 'We were now much less democrats than I had been, because so long as education continues to be so wretchedly imperfect, we dreaded the ignorance and especially the selfishness and brutality of the mass' (p. 138).

What Mill feared in democracy was less the type of government it might produce than the dominance, within society, of what he saw as a monolithic body of mediocre public opinion, which would be intolerant of dissent or even mere eccentricity. This was the chief preoccupation of his *On Liberty* (1859). It was because he saw public opinion, more than the state, as a threat to individual liberty that he had such apprehensions about the trend towards democracy. He wrote that 'the tyranny of the majority is now generally included among the evils against which society requires to be on its guard',[22] and that 'In politics it is almost a triviality to say that public opinion now rules the world'. Those groups who make up what is called public opinion are always 'a collective mediocrity' (p. 131). In much the same vein his contemporary Macaulay wrote that 'institutions purely democratic must, sooner or later, destroy liberty, or civilization, or both'.[23] The idea of democracy as a threat to liberty was not new, as we have seen; but it was to play a central role in modern liberal thinking about democracy.

Mill's fears led him eventually to favour proposals to give the educated more votes than the mass of the people.[24] All, including women, were to have one vote, but the educated were to have more in proportion to the level of their education; this, Mill believed, would provide a safeguard against the ignorance, selfishness and brutality which he so feared in the mass of the people. There was a streak of Platonic elitism in Mill. His perennial concern was to reconcile the general principle of democracy with the idea of government and social leadership being safely in the hands of an elite of the best and most enlightened members of society. Parliament and government should be elected by popular vote, or a weighted version of it, but once elected, the people should accept that an assembly of 'the best and wisest men in the nation' will make better decisions than the people themselves. Mill, unlike the radical democrats, did not therefore favour short parliaments. Anything less than five years would only encourage a 'timid subserviency' of representatives to their constituents:

> The idea of a rational democracy is, not that the people themselves govern, but that they have security for good government ... the best government (need it be said?) must be the government of the wisest, and these must always be a few.[25]

What gives the game away, of course, is that qualifying adjective 'rational'.

In Britain these anxieties, warnings and qualifications intensified in the period of debate that preceded the 1867 Reform Act. Perhaps the key figure in opening up that debate, and reviving the issue of the franchise, was John Bright, at least before Gladstone's conversion to the cause. Yet Bright, who was known as a radical liberal, famous for his attacks on the old aristocratic and feudal order, was emphatic that he was not a democrat: 'I do not pretend myself to be a democrat. I never accepted that title, and I believe those who knew me and spoke honestly of me never applied it to me.' And in the Commons in 1860 he declared: 'I have never uttered a word in favour of universal franchise either in this House or elsewhere.'[26] If even a radical liberal felt obliged to make such disavowals it may seem paradoxical to suggest that what was being discussed was, in fact, democracy. But however modest the proposed immediate reform might be, it was rightly seen that large issues of principle were raised by the direction in which society and the political system were moving.

Except, as we have seen, for confident bourgeois like James Mill and Edward Miall, both those who campaigned for universal suffrage, like the Chartists in the 1830s and 1840s, and those who dreaded and opposed it were agreed that it would lead to the political domination of the working class. That class would vote solidly as a class for candidates representative of itself, and since it made up a clear majority of the population, what could stand in the way of its political ascendancy? Robert Lowe, one of the bitterest opponents of the 1867 Act, warned: 'Once give working men the votes, and the machinery is ready to launch those votes in one compact mass upon the institutions and property of this country.'[27] Probably the main reason for the reconciliation of the middle and upper classes to the gradual extension of the franchise was that this never happened. The male working-class vote was, from the start, divided between the existing parties, and when socialist or social democratic parties appeared on the scene they seldom attained the political dominance which the solid support of the workers would have assured for them. Nevertheless, in the nineteenth century democracy was seen, by both its champions and its detractors, as a class issue. Hence the fierceness with which it was both fought for and resisted.

But then a truly epoch-making change in public attitudes took place. Some time between the moment when John Bright indignantly denied being a democrat and the early twentieth century

there was a reversal of official and public attitudes towards democracy. From being a principle which all but the most radical or
'extremist' were anxious to disown, it became one which all but
the most reactionary claimed to believe in. By the 1920s when
Mussolini, partly influenced by the elite theorists, proclaimed his
scornful opposition to democracy, such a position marked you out
as one who resisted the broad tendency of all politics since 1789.
How and why did this extraordinary and extraordinarily rapid turn-
about in attitudes take place?

I do not know of any study of this change which can answer that
question in anything like a precise and well-documented fashion.
The most popular suggestion is that it was the First World War, and
in particular the huge sacrifices of men in the Battle of the Somme
and the other slaughters on the Western Front, which made the
change of attitude, or rhetoric, necessary. To talk simply of empires
and patriotic duty was sensed to be no longer convincing as a public
justification for these sacrifices. The liberal democratic rhetoric
of President Woodrow Wilson suited the occasion far better.
'Sacrifices could be demanded in the name of democracy which
could not be expected for mere patriotism for the social order as it
was.'[28] But it was also, in a sense, an adjustment to reality. The vote
for all adult men at least was becoming more and more widely
established; yet there was still resistance to the idea of 'democracy'.
Might it not be better to bow to the inevitable, as Tocqueville had
suggested long before, and accept democracy in its limited
representative forms as a framework within which as much as
possible of the traditional structure of power and values should be
preserved?

This is not to say that the twentieth century saw the total disappearance of open opposition to democracy. Fascists like Mussolini were outspoken in their contempt for democracy:

> Fascism denies that the majority, through the mere fact of being a
> majority, can rule human societies . . . By democratic regimes we mean
> those in which from time to time the people is given the illusion of
> being sovereign, while true effective sovereignty lies in other, perhaps
> irresponsible and secret, forces. . . . Fascism rejects in democracy the
> absurd conventional lie of political equalitarianism . . .

Yet even Mussolini, or his ghost-writer Gentile, paid lip-service to
the term by defining Fascism in the next sentence as 'organized,
centralized, authoritarian democracy'.[29]

For the most part, however, those who in this century have dis-
liked or feared democracy, at least in the sense of popular power,
have found more subtle and sophisticated ways of formulating
these traditional sentiments. Instead of talking openly about 'the
mob' or 'the common herd' (J.S. Mill) or 'the swinish multitude'
(Burke), modern elitists have talked about 'the masses' and 'mass
society', and have even drawn a distinction between 'mass democracy' and 'liberal democracy'. Thus William Kornhauser, in *The
Politics of Mass Society* (1960), contended that 'Mass politics in
democratic society is therefore anti-democratic, since it contra-
venes the constitutional order'.[30] Another American writer, Walter
Lippmann, argued that in the liberal democracies 'mass opinion'
had come to dominate over governments, and that this represented
'a functional derangement of the relationship between the mass of
the people and the government'.[31] He wrote of 'the need to protect
the executive and judicial powers from the representative
assemblies and from mass opinion' (p. 45). Democracy, it seems,
had gone too far. The people, or 'the masses', had usurped powers
and functions which properly belonged to government and the
state. Lippmann's view, like J.S. Mill's, was that the electors have
the right to choose their rulers or government, but beyond that they
should leave government to govern without interference or
pressure: 'Their duty is to fill the office and not to direct the office-
holder' (p. 46). A not dissimilar view was put forward by Bernard
Crick, who said of referenda, the power to recall representatives
and other devices for popular intervention: 'They forget that the
first business of government is to govern . . . Government alone can
establish priorities of real social effort and actual policies. Democracy can only advise and consent, and then only in an indirect and
spasmodic manner.'[32]

The principal theoretical basis for these attempts to limit the role
of 'the masses' within the political system lay in the revision of
traditional democratic theory in such a way as to incorporate some
of the findings of modern political sociology, and some of the
arguments of the classical elite theorists, Pareto, Mosca and
Michels. The core of elite theory was the contention that democracy, in the strict traditional sense of rule by the people, is impossible: all government is government by an elite, or at best one among
a number of competing elites. The democratic aspiration in its
classical form is doomed – an outcome which is viewed with either
glee or regret according to the political orientation of the theorists

concerned. Raymond Aron expressed this conclusion succinctly: 'there is government *for* the people; there is no government *by* the people'.[33]

There was not much evidence of regret among the writers who then decided to rewrite democratic theory in order to incorporate the central elitist proposition. Without always being as explicit as writers like Lippmann, it seemed that most of them were content to redefine democracy in such a way as to eliminate its traditional popular participatory aspirations. They were thus able to get the best of both worlds. They could claim to be defending democracy while simultaneously denouncing the very tendencies and aspirations which had led their less sophisticated predecessors to condemn or criticize democracy as such.[34]

Probably the most influential text in the development of the modern elitist theory of democracy (or, alternatively, theory of democratic elitism) was Joseph Schumpeter's *Capitalism, Socialism and Democracy* (1942). Schumpeter drastically narrowed the conception of democracy he used by defining it as 'a political method ... for arriving at political – legislative and administrative – decisions', and therefore, he said, 'incapable of being an end in itself'.[35] He rapidly concluded that the classical ideal of government by the people was not only impossible but also undesirable on account of the proven ignorance, irrationality and apathy of the people. Furthermore, the traditional theory of democracy did not allow for 'a proper recognition of the vital fact of leadership' (p. 270). Given all these considerations, some supposedly empirical, but others more clearly normative, Schumpeter concluded that the proper role of the people was to choose their rulers through competitive elections, and then leave them to get on with the business of governing. The voters 'must understand that, once they have elected an individual, political action is his business and not theirs. This means that they must refrain from instructing him about what he is to do' (p. 295). This was, of course, in the tradition of Burke's response to his electors in Bristol nearly two centuries earlier. By this route Schumpeter arrived at his much quoted definition of what he termed 'the democratic method': 'that institutional arrangement for arriving at political decisions in which individuals acquire the power to decide by means of a competitive struggle for the people's vote' (p. 269).

Some of those who followed in Schumpeter's footsteps in the 1950s went even further in minimizing the popular role in a democratic system of politics. Thus S.M. Lipset wrote: 'The distinctive and most valuable element of democracy is the formation of a political elite in the competitive struggle for the vote of a mainly passive electorate.' The passivity of the electorate, so far from being a cause for concern or even regret, was viewed with positive approval: 'The belief that a very high level of participation is always good for democracy is not valid', Lipset magisterially announced.[36] Too much popular interest or activity could lead to what Kornhauser called 'mass movements subversive of liberty and of democracy itself' (p. 129). Edward Shils contended that 'pluralistic politics' was 'marked . . . by the moderation of political involvement', and prohibited 'emotional intensity'.[37] Others went further still, and suggested that political apathy might 'reflect the health of democracy' (Lipset), or praised it as 'a more or less effective counter-force to the fanatics who constitute the real danger to liberal democracy'.[38]

Another central plank in this revisionist argument was that there was no such thing as the popular will. All these writers, and many others, stressed what Crick termed 'the essential perception that all known advanced societies are inherently pluralistic and diverse' (p. 62). If this is so, then any attempts to conjure up a single popular will can only be factitious, and dangerous to the rights of individuals and groups within society: hence, in part, the suspicion with which mass political movements are viewed from within this perspective. Given the pluralistic nature of society, they can only be the product of hysteria and demagogic manipulation. But how was this pluralism to be embodied in the electoral process? The obvious answer would seem to be: through a plurality of parties, so that any government would have to be a coalition representative of at least a significant number of these diverse interests and groupings. The revisionist theorists were also, however, much concerned with strong and stable government. Many of them therefore tended to favour the single-party governments produced by two-party-dominated systems of the American or British type rather than coalition governments, however accurately the latter might reflect the 'pluralistic and diverse' character of society.

A way out of this dilemma was found by elevating interest and pressure groups to a central role in the new version of democracy. These are the groups and organizations which express the vast diversity of interests within society. It is the business of government to listen to them, mediate between them, and evolve the compromise settlements which will take account of all 'legitimate' concerns and interests in so far as this is possible. John Plamenatz announced enthusiastically that 'the voice of the people is heard everlastingly' through the spokespersons of these organizations, and Robert Dahl believed in the 1950s that the United States possessed 'a political system in which all the active and legitimate groups in the population can make themselves heard at some critical stage in the process of decision'.[39] Through pressure and interest groups it could be claimed that the old democratic principle of participation was reinstated, but in a suitably modern form which accepted that this possibility existed for groups but not for individuals.

In the twentieth century, then, 'the century of the common man' as it was once called, misgivings about democracy did not vanish. They may even have intensified as the franchise was extended and the character of politics changed accordingly. But they did not usually involve a direct challenge to the principle of democracy: that has ceased to be a politically acceptable position in most parts of the world. Instead, the definition of democracy itself has been revised, adapted, narrowed and diluted to render it compatible with the persisting belief in the necessity or the virtue of rule by elites, with an equally persistent mistrust of 'the masses'; and, perhaps most important of all, to render it compatible with the existing political systems of the Western world which call themselves 'democracies'. Given this revised definition, it becomes natural to talk about preserving and defending democracy rather than achieving it, for of course it already exists in such fortunate countries as Britain and the United States.

By proclaiming the arrival of democracy, and with it 'the end of ideology' and ideological politics, the revisionists of the 1950s perhaps hoped to bring to an end the perennial debate about democracy. Instead, and predictably, they provoked a renewal of that debate. Their attempts to abandon many of the ideas and ideals of classical democratic theory were immediately challenged by other theorists; while their celebrations of actually existing democracies founded on lukewarm politics and 'a mainly passive electorate' were countered by the marked revival of popular activity and radical commitment which was already taking off in the late 1950s when these texts were being written and published. Fresh demands for participation were put forward, and these generated fresh discussion about this supposedly obsolete concept. Trends towards the centralization and bureaucratization of power, far from being accepted with resignation, generated an opposition which stressed the virtues of smallness, accessibility, openness and decentralization. Globalization, and in particular the concentration of economic power in ways which transcended national boundaries and mocked the authority of elected governments, only renewed and strengthened this oppositional tendency. This opposition has not been coherent or coordinated, and is still much weaker than the centripetal trends it opposes. But, like the work of one of its ancestors, Rousseau, it strikes a chord which reverberates widely among those who feel themselves to be increasingly powerless, and resent it.

What, then, are the prospects for democracy in the opening years of the twenty-first century? An optimistic view of recent developments might suggest that the nemesis of Communism and the world-wide reverberations of this crash marked also the beginning of the global triumph of the democratic principle. All the ex-Communist countries of eastern Europe have now staged elections and are governed by elected executives of one kind or another (although this is not true of all the constituent nation-states of the former Soviet Union). And the end of these one-party states has undermined similar structures elsewhere. Elections have been instituted in countries as disparate as South Africa, Chile, Nicaragua, Zambia, Angola and Cambodia, and in some cases their authenticity has been proven by their result – the dislodgement of the incumbent regime – as in Nicaragua and Zambia.

Right-wing regimes also crumbled. General Pinochet of Chile was destroyed by the negative result of a referendum on his own presidency, in which he was the only permitted candidate! The Marcos regime in the Philippines was replaced by an elected presidency. Most important of all, in South Africa white supremacy was replaced at long last by black majority rule. In the 1970s Portugal and Spain both emerged from long periods of dictatorship and established parliamentary-electoral systems with remarkable smoothness. It was part of the same southern European pattern that at the same time Greece shook off one more episode of military dictatorship, and with it the monarchy, and established a democratic republic.

These momentous developments could perhaps be interpreted as a global movement, or at least drift, towards democracy, or popular election, as the most stable and acceptable basis for government.

And I think there is some basis for optimism. With the exception – and it is a very large and significant exception – of the growing numbers of Islamic fundamentalists, for whom the only legitimate government is one which implements shariah (divine) law, popular election has increasingly come to be seen as the most, or even the sole, legitimate basis for any government. This is not to say that elected governments will necessarily be of a parliamentary character, nor that they will pursue liberal policies. The elections that were aborted in Algeria in 1992 might have produced an Islamic government bent on imposing Muslim law and custom on a widely Westernized society – which is why they were cancelled, with dire and predictable results in terms of civil strife.

The end of the dictatorships in Greece and Iberia in the 1970s can plausibly be seen as a definitive end to the long struggle in southern Europe between right-wing authoritarianism and liberal and progressive forces. Only a super-optimist would offer a comparable analysis of recent developments in central and eastern Europe. The absence of past experience of democratic politics in countries such as Russia and Poland (as opposed to the Czech Republic), coupled with vast economic problems as well as ethnic and border disputes, all offer fertile ground for a return to one form or another of authoritarian rule. Those who talk glibly of 'free market democracy', as if the former were necessarily accompanied by the latter, expect that we will overlook the many countries in which capitalism and dictatorship go, or have gone, hand in hand. Western capitalism has been eager to integrate the former Communist countries into the global capitalist market, and economic advisers and speculators have flooded into eastern Europe. As might be expected, a lot less effort has been devoted to helping these countries to set up sturdy democratic institutions and customs. The consequence is that the combination of capitalism with authoritarian government, familiar in Latin America, parts of Africa and east Asia, is being reproduced in Russia, Ukraine and some other former Soviet republics. The blind eye which is consistently turned towards Chinese repression and authoritarianism suggests that it is the opening up of the Communist and ex-Communist societies as markets for sales and investment, rather than the struggle to create democracy, which really excites active Western interest.

On the one hand, therefore, we can take some comfort from the increasing acceptance of the minimal democratic principle that governments should be popularly elected as *the* test of legitimacy for any regime or political system. Democracy is not about to be submerged beneath a wave of overt authoritarianism, as was feared in the mid-twentieth century. It may even be that the most powerful ideologically based forms of non-democratic authoritarianism are now either dead or discredited and doomed.

On the other hand, dictatorship or military rule very often does not trouble to disguise or justify itself with much in the way of ideology. The rule of force is readily justified by reference to the need for order, the danger of subversion, and so forth. As has been suggested already in this book, hostility to democracy has by no means vanished from contemporary politics. There are plenty of powerful and privileged groups who see democracy as a threat to themselves and their values, and will therefore resist its development by every means, including violence and repression when these are judged to be necessary and effective. There are those, too, for whom democracy and the freedoms which often accompany it are an inconvenience, an obstruction to the uninhibited pursuit of wealth and profit, and who therefore welcome that combination of free markets and authoritarianism to which I have just referred. It is this capitalist authoritarianism which poses one of the greatest obstacles to the development and spread of democracy in this post-Communist period.

# PART TWO

# Ideas

# 5
# Government by
# the People

Having taken a brief and summary view of the history of democracy, and the opposition to it, it is time to return to the question of definition, which a historical perspective should help to clarify. Earlier in this book it was suggested that the notion of 'popular power' could be seen as the core of the various ideas and conceptions of democracy. The reason for doing this should now be a little clearer: although democracy has often been equated with a system of government, or recently even more narrowly with a method of choosing a government, too much stress on government diverts attention from one of the most constant aspirations behind the idea of democracy – the desire to bridge, or even to abolish, the gap between government and the governed, state and society implicit in so much conventional political thinking.

What is now called 'direct' democracy, as practised in ancient Athens, did to an astonishing extent abolish the distinction. The large numbers involved in the various institutions of decision-taking and law-making, the principle of (usually annual) rotation among office-holders, and the choice of members of these bodies by lot rather than election, all ensured that participation was not confined to a minority of activists but was spread across the whole citizen body. Similarly, it was Rousseau's conviction that no one could be truly free who did not govern him- or herself, and that therefore only some kind of direct democracy provided the framework within which government and freedom could be reconciled. It was for this reason that in *Du Contrat Social* he mocked the English by contending that the English people 'is free only during the election of Members of Parliament; as soon as the Members are elected, the people is enslaved; it is nothing' (Book I, Ch. 15).[1] Once you transfer your right to self-government to someone else, even if that person is deemed to be your 'representative', you are no longer free. The doctrine of parliamentary sovereignty was illegitimate, if not incomprehensible, to Rousseau. For him sovereignty belonged inalienably to the people. The problem was to decide how they could retain it and exercise it.

That is what democracy was originally understood to mean: the people governing themselves, without mediation through chosen representatives, directly or, if necessary, by the rotation of governing offices among the citizens. Many modern commentators, from Burke, Hamilton and Madison to the present day, have frankly seen the device of representation as a means of limiting popular participation and control, and of retaining the day-to-day powers of government in the hands of a (preferably enlightened) elite. There may be a case for such a restraint upon popular power, but it cannot be a democratic one. The democratic argument in relation to representation was very different. Typically it was justified, by Paine and James Mill, for example, simply as a means of adapting the democratic principle to large and populous societies. Consequently, their concern was to prevent elected representatives from acquiring too much independent power or becoming a permanent self-perpetuating oligarchy. This was the purpose of such proposals as annual or biennial elections, a prohibition on any representative serving for more than two consecutive terms, single-chamber legislatures, and so on. The intention was that the substance of popular power be retained as far as possible.

The closer a community comes to realizing the democratic ideal of self-government, the greater the extent of citizen participation in government, the more the conventional distinction between government and governed is dissolved. In such circumstances to categorize democracy simply as a form or method of government is misleading. It is true, of course, that self-government is one answer to the problem of government (who governs?), but it is not simply or solely that. In such circumstances the state is socialized and society is politicized. Participatory democracy necessarily has implications for social life, and is better regarded as a way of life, and a way of running a whole society, than as a mere political device or method. This was the message of Pericles' famous funeral speech, quoted on p. 23.

It is noticeable that even a writer like J.S. Mill, for all his apprehensions about public opinion and mass ignorance, never abandoned the basic democratic principle that as far as possible the people should govern themselves, and that therefore the ultimate objective had to be the maximum of direct, personal participation:

> it is evident that the only government which can fully satisfy all the exigencies of the social state is one in which the whole people participate; that any participation, even in the smallest public function, is useful; that the participation should everywhere be as great as the general degree of improvement of the community will allow; and that nothing less can be ultimately desirable than the admission of all to a share in the sovereign power of the state.[2]

It was only in the twentieth century that theorists attempted to produce a version of democracy in which popular participation was treated with suspicion, if not regarded as positively undesirable. This represented a fundamental departure from the traditional understanding of what democracy is, or was. Whether it was approved or not – and usually it was not – until then it was understood on all sides that democracy meant, to a lesser or greater degree, popular power, popular sovereignty, popular participation. There is no good reason why that traditional understanding should now be abandoned, however inconvenient it may be for some of those who would otherwise like to shelter under the umbrella of the term 'democracy'.

We need also to ask whether the confinement of the democratic principle to the government of the state really meets the aspirations which democracy was intended to realize. The belief that democracy meant government by the people, or at least by their accountable representatives, was premised on the assumption that governmental power was *the* power in society, that politics dominated over social and economic life, and that no factional power or interest group could successfully resist the legitimate might of the popular will. Legitimate state authority meant power. The idea that there could be such authority without effective power hardly occurred to anyone.

But now we are ever more aware that the power of governments, including elected governments, is being bypassed and dwarfed by the huge economic and political power of the great transnational corporations and conglomerates. Their decisions and policies can determine the pattern of prosperity or poverty in many countries far more drastically than anything governments can do. And this not only undermines the legitimacy of elected governments; it generates apathy and cynicism about politics as a whole.

One of the paradoxes of contemporary political thinking is that while much conventional theory has tried to restrict the idea of democracy to that of choosing a government from competing elites, it is also widely admitted that the theoretical sovereignty of these 'democratic' governments is not matched by their actual powers over society. If so much power lies outside the domain or the control of elected governments, it is surely odd to hold that the requirements of democracy are met when government alone is popularly elected and, in principle, accountable. Certainly the reputation of democracy is diminished when its application appears to be so restricted and its outcome so ineffectual. Here we have a further reason why defining democracy simply in terms of government is unsatisfactory.

In Britain, as elsewhere, the imbalance between non-elected powers and elected and accountable local authorities has been systematically increased in recent years. The role of elected councillors on such bodies as police and health authorities has been reduced, many of their powers have been taken over by central government, and in many cities agencies such as 'urban development corporations' have been created with wide-ranging powers that enable them to bypass elected local authorities altogether. Whatever may be said in favour of such developments, they are certainly not democratic. And if we hold to the idea of democracy as popular power, then clearly the concentration of so much power in non-accountable hands, outside the control of elected bodies, is incompatible with democracy. Far from being outdated, this old and broad conception of democracy holds out the only hope of compensating for the weaknesses of elected representative assemblies, dwarfed as they presently are by the bureaucratic and monopolistic structures of power which surround them.

In Britain only 59 per cent of eligible voters bothered to cast a vote in the 2001 general election, and this steep decline from normal levels of electoral participation, which had been between 70 and 80 per cent, caused much anxious discussion. Many Members of Parliament were themselves worried about the declining status and effectiveness of Parliament, officially the sovereign elected authority in the British political system. Much government had been passed into the hands of 'agencies', and other institutions for which no minister accepted any direct responsibility, and which were therefore difficult if not impossible to call to account. There were some politicians and commentators who welcomed developments of this kind, and hailed the end of 'big government'. But the popular response seems to have been that if elected representatives and government count for so little, then there is no very strong reason for taking much interest in them – which is logical enough, but clearly dangerous for the health of a democracy.

'Popular power' and 'government by the people' are not, I would suggest, vacuous slogans, but it is easy for critics and sceptics to dismiss them as mere rhetoric so long as those who use them fail to specify what they imply, in practice and in some detail. That must be our next task, within the limits of available space. What is government by the people? Or what can it be in the context of large-scale modern societies? Does talk about 'the will of the people' still – if it ever did – make sense? Can any sizeable society have a 'general will' or a general interest?

Let us leave aside, for the moment, the practical difficulties which stand or are believed to stand in the way of direct democracy. Even if there was personal participation by all the citizens in the making of decisions and policies, the only situation in which it would even appear to be clear what was the will of the people would be a unanimous decision. Unanimity, or the next best thing, a decision which no one actually opposes, is not unknown, especially in relatively small groups or communities. But the larger the body, the rarer it becomes. And however desirable may be the achievement of unanimity, at least on basic values and the general directions to be pursued by a society, it is unwise, in any diverse society, to make it a rule or a requirement. For then, as Professor Jack Lively pointed out, any minority, or even a single individual, might block a decision or policy which otherwise commands overwhelming support.[3] It could hardly be argued that to place the power of veto in the hands of an individual or a minority is a democratic device, except perhaps in certain very unusual and specific circumstances.

Some writers, as we have seen, are suspicious of unanimity on the grounds that it can only be, or is at least most likely to be, the product of either manipulation from above or the coercive pressure of majority opinion on the rest, or of a combination of both of these. There are certainly occasions of which this is true. But even when unanimity is the genuine product of a free decision on the part of all, it still poses some problems. These problems are raised, from very different angles, by Rousseau and Bentham.

Bentham was notoriously sceptical of all notions of 'community', 'general interest' and the like:

> The community is a fictitious body, composed of the individual per-
> sons who are considered as constituting as it were its members. The
> interest of the community then is, what? – the sum of the interests of
> the several members who compose it.[4]

But in fact it is not necessarily the case that if each person votes, or
decides, according to what he or she perceives as his or her personal
interest or wishes, the outcome is the good of all or even of the
majority. Some good examples of this are given by Fred Hirsch in
*Social Limits to Growth*. Suppose that post-school education is
seen, plausibly enough, as the key to a career and social advance-
ment; then all parents will want their children to have it. Proposals
for the expansion of post-school education are therefore likely to
command majority support. But the greater the number of people
who obtain post-school education, the less likely it is to provide
them with entry to a career. As Hirsch puts it:

> If everyone stands on tiptoe, no one sees better. Where social inter-
> action of this kind is present, individual action is no longer a sure
> means of fulfilling individual choice: the preferred outcome may be
> attainable only through collective action.

It is an example of what he calls 'the modern conflict between individualistic actions and satisfaction of individualistic preferences.
Getting what one wants is increasingly divorced from doing as one
likes.'[5] So even unanimous decisions, taken by individuals freely
acting according to their perception of their own interests, will not
necessarily produce the result they want.

Rousseau understood this, and that is one reason why he wished
to distinguish between the will of all and what he called 'the general
will'. What we all want as individuals is not, in sum, the same as
what we want as a community. Even unanimity does not guarantee
that the general or common good prevails. Rousseau was keenly
aware that majority decisions, or even unanimous ones, are not
necessarily right – right, that is, not only according to the moral
criteria of any particular individual but from the point of view of
the good of the community itself. This did not lead him to question
the principle of majority decisions; but it did lead him to pay attention to the social, cultural and economic conditions in which the will
of all, or the will of the majority, would be more rather than less
likely to coincide with 'the general will'. Rousseau uses this term to
mean what all of us would will if we thought of ourselves not as

private individuals but as citizens identifying ourselves with the good of the community.

Rousseau as a theorist of democracy has attracted a great deal of hostile commentary, in particular from writers who see 'totalitarian' implications in *Du Contrat Social*, or even a blueprint for what has been termed 'totalitarian democracy'. They find in Rousseau's stress on the unity of society, and his dislike of factions or interest groups, a threat to the pluralism and tolerance of diversity which are regarded as the hallmarks of a *liberal* democracy. But these critics do not always ask themselves whether any society may not need a degree of unity in order to be a society at all, or how much diversity even a liberal society can tolerate without falling apart.[6] Rousseau's dislike of 'sectional associations' sprang from what he saw as the growing tendency for people to identify themselves primarily with these associations and their interests rather than with the community as a whole, and so to forget their duties as citizens. This is a shrewd observation, and one which is highly relevant to modern pluralist societies. Perhaps it is only because the duties of citizenship have been reduced to a minimum in those societies, with even voting being voluntary in most of them, that they survive as unitary states at all.

So although a voluntary unanimity among participating citizens could certainly be regarded as an authentic expression of what all wanted as individuals, even that would not in itself ensure the realization of the general good or the general interest. Here is one of the problems of democracy to which we shall have to return. But for the moment it is enough to recognize that even unanimity can have its problematic aspects; and, since unanimity is so rarely achieved on a large scale, we need to consider next the next best thing, the principle with which democracy is very often crudely identified: majority decision-taking or majority rule.

# Majority Rule and its Problems

Is it reasonable, in the absence of unanimity, to equate the will of the people with the will of the majority, as is so often done in every-day politics? To see what is at stake here, we can juxtapose this question with two others directed at the same problem. Is there any reason why the minority, or any minority, should not be accounted part of the people? Or is there any sense in which those who oppose and vote against a particular policy or decision can be said to assent to it, or can be said to be governing themselves when they have voted against the policy that has been adopted?

Spokespersons for the majority have often tried to portray the minority who oppose as not really being part of 'the people' at all. The idea of 'the people' has often had class connotations, which meant that aristocrats or bourgeois were excluded from the defi-nition of 'the people', as was the case with Sieyès. Now it may be quite legitimate to point out that this or that minority group has vested interests which run counter to the interest or good of the great majority. But it is quite another thing to go on to suggest that such a minority therefore possesses no political rights, or should be deprived of those which it holds equally with all other citizens. I can see nothing in democratic thinking which allows us to think of 'the people' as anything other than the whole body of citizens, minori-ties as well as majorities, those who oppose and dissent as well as those who belong to the dominant majority. To equate the will of the people with the will of the majority may often be a justifiable piece of political shorthand; but those in a minority, whether it be on a particular issue or in a more long-term and fundamental way, are always entitled to remind the rest of society that they too are part of 'the people'. What can happen when the majority forget this, or try to deny it, has been seen in Northern Ireland over the past thirty years and more.

As for the position of the minority in relation to the democratic principle of self-government, Rousseau poses the issue as starkly as anyone:

> yet it may be asked how a man can be at once free and forced to conform to wills which are not his own. How can the opposing minority be both free and subject to laws to which they have not consented?
>
> *Du Contrat Social* (Book IV, Ch. 2)

The short, blunt answer to this question (which is not the answer that Rousseau gives) is that they cannot. The minority is not governing itself; it is being governed by the majority. It is therefore not free in the fundamental sense which is Rousseau's starting point. It is hard to see a way out of this impasse. So long as there is a need for collective decision-making and for policies which give direction to a whole community or society, and so long as or whenever unanimity cannot be achieved, it is hard to see what alternative there can be to the minority being compelled to go along with the decision of the majority. As Locke put it, in justifying rule by the majority, a community 'being one body must move one way'. A community can tolerate much diversity – more than in Locke's day when religious conformity was one requirement for full citizenship – but any society has to have some common rules and policies, whether it be in matters as trivial as which side of the road we drive on or as momentous as whether there is capital punishment. The democratic principle must be that, where there cannot be universal agreement, matters should be settled according to the will or wishes of the majority.

It is this impasse which has led Robert Paul Wolff, taking Rousseau's question as his starting point, to conclude that the only kind of society in which the freedom, or moral autonomy, of every individual is preserved is, in fact, one without government, an anarchist society.[1] It is a powerful argument, as was demonstrated by the heated responses it provoked. But it does not invalidate the argument of the last paragraph: so long as we judge there to be a need for government and common policies, democratic principle will require that minorities have to accept majority decisions to which they are opposed.

It is possible, though, to make too much of this undoubtedly awkward fact. Although we cannot honestly say that those who unsuccessfully oppose a particular decision or policy consent to that decision or policy when it is carried out despite their opposition, we can say that they are nevertheless bound by that decision in so far as they accept both the principle of majority decisions and the fairness of the procedures through which the decision is reached or the policy made. If you accept that unanimity is a near impossibility, and that a majority decision is the next best thing, you also have to accept, as a general rule, that you will abide by a majority decision when it turns out that you are among the minority. It is in this sense that a system of majority decision-taking, rather than any particular decision, can be said to be based on consent. And so long as all citizens stand a good chance of being among the majority on at least some of the major and significant issues, most if not all will be content to accept the majority principle. They will not feel that the principle discriminates against them.

But there are many states and societies where, unfortunately, this is not the case. If a society is so divided that it contains within itself one or more permanent minorities, who know that on the issues that matter most to them they can never hope to get their way, precisely because of the operation of the majority principle, then that principle ceases to be adequate. The existence of permanent minorities, whose aspirations, wishes and even principles are systematically ignored or overridden in the collective decision-making processes, can easily make a majoritarian democracy unjust and unworkable. The strict mathematical equality of each person's vote with all others conceals the fact that in such circumstances some votes carry no weight or impact at all. At one time such excluded or impotent minorities tended to be religious. Today they are more likely to be national or ethnic. In Northern Ireland that minority was both religious and national.

Northern Ireland has provided a particularly clear illustration of the sometimes hidden problems involved in majoritarian thinking about democracy. One such concealed question is *which* majority, if any, ought to be the decisive one. In other words, which is the group or 'constituency' which ought to take the vital decisions, and within which the majority view ought to prevail? As was noted earlier, past elections in Northern Ireland itself always produced clear majorities in favour of Unionist government. Despite this, the result was a travesty of democracy in that the permanent minority of Catholics and Irish nationalists were excluded from the Protestant Unionist conception of 'the people', called in this case 'the people of Ulster'. The votes of the minority did not count as the clear expression of a minority opinion; they did not count at all in the eyes of the majority except as evidence of Catholic disloyalty to the Northern semi-state.

So there has been oppression of the minority in Northern Ireland. One response to this has been to challenge the position of the majority in the province by suggesting that it is not the population of the province who should decide the issues at stake but the population of the whole of Ireland. This would immediately reverse the relative positions of majority and minority in Northern Ireland. Within Ireland as a whole the Protestants would constitute a clear minority, easily outweighed by the Catholic and nationalist majority in Ireland as a whole. From a democratic point of view this would, of course, be no improvement if the will of the Protestant minority then similarly counted for nothing in that larger context. There is a third possible grouping within which the majoritarian principle might be applied, and that is the United Kingdom as a whole. Within that constituency too, the Unionists are only a small minority. But since the official essence of Unionism is the claim that Northern Ireland is as integral a part of the United Kingdom as Yorkshire or Suffolk, it is hard to see on what grounds of principle the Unionists could object to their fate being decided by a majority within the United Kingdom as a whole. Yet of course they do.

The conflict over the future of Northern Ireland thus draws our attention to a rather neglected question in discussion of democracy: what is the group that has the right to decide a particular policy or issue, by a majority vote if necessary? And how can we decide between competing constituencies? Probably most British people think that the inhabitants of the Falkland Islands, or of Gibraltar, should decide what state should govern them. But that is certainly not the view of the Argentinians, or the Spanish. And it is not so obvious that they are wrong. Supposing Yorkshire or Cornwall decided by a majority vote to secede from Britain and elect their own government. Would the rest of Britain simply accept that their democratic right to self-determination was being exercised? It is very doubtful.

These questions arise insistently in relation to ethnic minorities within broader societies: does the majority in the society as a whole have the democratic right to decide on matters which particularly, or specifically, affect such minorities? But it also arises in relation to many conflicts between local interests or communities and a national government. Consider the following exchange between an opponent of nuclear waste dumping and a representative of the firm which had been authorized to do the dumping:

> 'Ninety thousand people in Bedfordshire have already signed a petition saying no to the dump. Isn't that enough?' Democracy, explained Mr McIverney, was all about the decisions of Parliament, and Parliament had granted his engineers permission to go on site.[2]

Leaving aside, for the moment, the identification of democracy with Parliament, clearly the democratic problem here is: who should decide? Is it the will of those most directly affected, the local community, which should determine the outcome, or the will of the nation as a whole, as expressed through the decisions of Parliament? There is no easy answer to such questions. Probably most people in Britain accept the need for a national network of motorways; but few if any specific communities welcome the construction of one on their doorstep. From a democratic point of view it is not self-evident, despite the claim of the spokesperson for Nirex, that central government decisions, supported in principle by a majority of the national population, should invariably override local majorities. In such circumstances the opinions and interests of those most directly affected ought to count for more than the opinions of those of us who are only marginally affected, if at all. We might well consider that the local majority, not the national one, is the one that ought to count for most.

How should we weigh the wishes of a majority of, for example, the people of Scotland or Quebec against the wishes of a majority of the British or Canadians as a whole? Constitutionally, it is often the larger grouping, or its elected representatives, which has the legal right to decide; but it is often that very constitutional situation to which the minority objects – not least because in its own territory, region or country it constitutes a majority. A sensitivity to the grievances, the self-respect, and even in some respects the autonomy of minorities is an essential attribute of variegated majorities which wish to hold any kind of plural society together. Thus Spain has managed to retain the allegiance of Catalans (if not of Basques) by accepting the legitimacy of Catalonia's distinctive character, institutions and language; and the devolution of limited powers of self-government to Wales and Scotland within Britain, recognizing the aspirations of a majority of those voting in referenda in both countries, is similarly intended to forestall the possible fragmentation of the United Kingdom.

There are therefore sound reasons for rejecting any crude equation of democracy with an unqualified principle of majority rule. 'The people' cannot be equated with only a majority of them, and 'government by the people' cannot be equated with government by the majority, let alone the representatives of the majority. Minorities are also part of the people, and, as far as possible, their interests, views and convictions must be taken into account in the processes of policy-making and decision-taking. Of course this is not always possible. Often compromise is not possible: a choice has to be made between diametrically opposed policies. But a democracy in which some groups, ethnic, religious or political, are permanently in a minority, and so in opposition, is likely to be unstable and may lose legitimacy. In extreme circumstances a minority, and especially a national minority, finding itself in such a position may simply decide to secede and create a society and state in which it forms the majority. This may yet happen with both Quebec and Scotland. One of the dangers of majoritarianism is that majorities are always apt to forget that in another context they might constitute a minority. Another is the easy assumption that in actual democratic politics the majority in each *existing* state should have the right to decide on all issues. Which majority is the relevant one, the one that ought to decide, is a question that always needs to be asked.

# Equality and the General Interest

Implicit in the foregoing discussion about the relations between majorities and minorities was a major question which must now be explicitly asked: how far does democracy require a foundation of shared values among all its citizens? Or, to put it another way, does the concept of the general interest or the general will have any part to play in democratic thinking? The consensus of modern liberal thinking has been that it does not; it has preferred to stress the 'inherently pluralistic and diverse' nature of modern societies, and the consequent need to reach a consensus or compromise among the various competing interests and groups within society. As a counter to crude majoritarianism, this is obviously valuable. It is salutary to be reminded that in many situations and many respects society is not simply divisible into two parts, the majority and the minority, but is in fact a conglomeration of minorities, none of which can have a democratic claim to dominate, and which must therefore learn to live with each other.

It often used to be said that Britain had a two-party political system, meaning by this not merely that the electoral system favoured the two major parties, but, less contentiously, that these two parties between them nearly monopolized the votes cast. Yet despite that, even in the 1950s neither the Conservatives nor Labour ever obtained an absolute majority of the votes, and today it is even clearer that there is no single majority party in British politics. Similarly, when we examine opinions on specific issues, it frequently turns out that no single position or policy commands majority support: opinion is divided amongst a range of options – although opinion polls, with their predilection for yes/no answers to unduly simple questions, often conceal this. In such circumstances, some kind of compromise or attempt to reach a consensus may often be the most democratic as well as the most prudent course.

But, as we have seen, there are many situations in which compromise is not possible, and some in which it is not desirable either. As Robert Paul Wolff pointed out in an acute critique of conventional pluralism, it is easier and more plausible to urge compromise when it is interests rather than principles which are in conflict.[1] If Roman Catholics believe that abortion is always wrong and contrary to God's law, there is no compromise they can be offered, or which they can accept, which will satisfy their principles. Or take capital punishment. Either you have it, or you don't. The issue can be resolved at different levels – within the United States some states have it, others do not – but there is, there can be, no half-way house, no compromise more or less acceptable to all.

Even with interests, it ought not to be casually assumed that all interests are automatically legitimate, or that compromises can and should be made to accommodate them. Aristotle was of the opinion that there would always be rich and poor within society, that their interests were naturally opposed, and that it was the business of government to persuade them to coexist, and to meet their legitimate demands. But nowadays not everyone is so ready to accept such divisions as unalterable, and if one holds the not unreasonable belief that the existence of wealth is one cause of poverty, then clearly we are faced with a more difficult choice: either to tolerate the existence of both wealth and poverty or to aim at abolishing poverty, in which case we have no option but to attack wealth. If there is a choice to be made between tolerating wealth and poverty and trying to create greater economic equality, then it is not immediately obvious that the former is the more democratic course. Indeed, I shall argue presently that there is a connection between democracy and social and economic equality. To confer legitimacy as a matter of course on all interests, even conflicting ones, is to run the risk of making democratic politics synonymous with a static paralysis in policy, or with what Thomas Carlyle called 'self-cancelling Donothingism' (*Chartism*, 1839).[2]

Nor ought it to be assumed that the spectrum of lobbies and special-interest groups represents all the proper and vital concerns of society, or that such concerns are properly embodied in balances and compromises between them. Indeed it is probably true to say, as a rough generalization, that the larger the concern, and the larger the number of people involved or affected, the less likely is it that the concern or interest will be represented accurately, or at all, within an interest-group system. The threat of nuclear destruction, for example, hangs over us all. Everyone is affected by the policies chosen to avert that threat, and nearly everyone is anxious and concerned about it to some degree. But how is that concern to be expressed? Not necessarily by supporting the Campaign for Nuclear Disarmament or some other 'peace' organization, since concern is not the same thing as supporting a particular policy for disarmament. Yet governments ought to resist the temptation to dismiss peace movements as representing only a minority opinion, for it is in the nature of a wider but vaguer anxiety about the issue that it can hardly be organized or form the basis of a coherent campaign.

The point becomes even clearer if we consider such concerns as health or education. Everyone is affected to some degree by the nature and quality of health and education provision in their society. There is, we might say, a general interest at stake here. Yet the best-organized and most influential lobbies and pressure groups in these areas represent, characteristically, professional group interests – doctors, nurses, teachers – or perhaps specific groups of long-term patients, the disabled, and so on. The interests of these groups may or may not be identical with the interests of the ordinary users of these services. How are those interests, the interests of all of us who may one day be patients of the health service, or who may become parents with children at school or at college, to be effectively represented? Such general concerns do not belong and do not fit into the straitjacket of a system of pressure-group lobbying and organization.

Yet such general concerns and interests are real and solid; they are not a Rousseauist fiction. And they are primary, not residual. Health services exist for the benefit of patients, not doctors; schools and colleges are for students, not for teachers or administrators. I believe, therefore, that Rousseau was right to look with apprehension on the fragmentation of society into a collection of interest groups, and to see that in such circumstances it is all too easy to lose sight of the general interest, the good of the community as a whole. That general interest is neither an amalgam of nor a compromise between the interests of various specific groups; nor, as we saw in our discussion of unanimity, can it be equated, in Benthamite fashion, with the sum of the choices of individuals, acting as individuals. For the good of the community as a whole to be realized, it is clearly necessary for people to think and act, not simply as self-interested individuals or as members of particular interest groups, but as citizens, as members of the community as a whole. Yet except in times of war or acute external threat, this seems rarely to happen in modern democratic societies. Is there any way in which the old classical republican spirit of citizenship can be revived under modern conditions?

Here again I believe that Rousseau's perceptions are still relevant. He believed that too great a degree of inequality within a society would prevent a common will or common interest from developing, and that is surely correct. Whereas in Aristotle's day, and indeed for some two thousand years afterwards, it might have been conceivable that extremes of wealth and poverty, and even of freedom and slavery, could coexist as part of a single society, by the time of Rousseau that was no longer the case. Consciousness of a conflict of interests, particularly on the part of the rich and propertied, had become too acute. That is even more clearly the case today. Governments, whether elected or not, who attempt large-scale improvements in the conditions of the poor and exploited will run headlong into the implacable opposition of the rich and privileged. Sometimes, as in Chile in 1973, this has led to the destruction of electoral democracy itself. It might be said that this was, in part, because the elected government of President Salvador Allende did not command sufficient support for its radical programme. That is unconvincing in my view. Even a government with substantial majority support would have encountered the same opposition. The rich are not normally inhibited in the defence of their own interests by the knowledge that they are only a small minority of the population.

Two possible conclusions can be drawn. The pessimistic conclusion is that electoral democracy can only survive by not tackling major social injustices and alienating powerful interest groups in society – in which case the poor will, in the long run, not consider democracy worth supporting. There are plenty of signs that this is already happening in Britain and, even more, in the United States. The eagerness of politicians to placate the rich, and the close links between wealth and government, convince many at the bottom of society that it is not worth voting: 'politics has nothing to offer us'. The alternative conclusion is that if democracy is not to be immobilized it must be founded on a substantial degree of social and economic equality – that is, on the existence of a real and concrete common interest in society. This is hardly an optimistic conclusion either, since the problem remains of how such equality is to be created if not by elected government itself. Nevertheless, without the sense of a common interest, clearly democracy itself is at risk, whether from a privileged minority determined to obstruct policies aimed at helping the poor majority, or, as in Northern Ireland, from the forcible incorporation into the state of a minority who do not accept the legitimacy of that state and who are then systematically excluded from power and influence.

Democracy does not imply a limitless diversity within society. It needs a foundation not only of shared values but also of shared experience, so that people identify with the political system to which they belong, and can trust its procedures and their outcomes. This means not only that those procedures are seen and felt to be fair. It is also necessary that no significant minorities feel themselves to be permanently excluded from power or influence; that groups and individuals sense that they are roughly equal in their ability to influence the outcome of communal policy-making; and that those outcomes embody what people recognize to be the general interests of society rather than merely a combination or balance of the interests of various particular and organized groups or specific interests.

This therefore brings me to the second reason why democracy is bound up with a measure of economic and social equality. Inequalities of that kind, if they are gross and excessive, not only threaten the coherence of society, but also tend to negate the principle of political equality of which democracy is an expression. There is, in other words, no neat or clear distinction to be drawn between political equality and social and economic equality. The belief that political equality was attained by the establishment of universal suffrage was based on the assumption, mentioned earlier, that governments were indeed sovereign over society, and that ultimately nothing could prevent a popularly elected government from carrying out its mandate. This sociologically naive view has long since had to be abandoned. Nobody now supposes that political processes begin and end with elections, or that elected governments have a monopoly of political power. So the question for democracy is whether, outside the franchise, political power, the power to affect governmental policies and priorities, is spread evenly and equally across society. As we have seen, some of the earlier and more enthusiastic apologists for pluralism, such as Dahl and Plamenatz, did suggest both that the spread of pressure and interest groups covered more or less the whole of society and also that such groups competed with each other on a roughly equal basis. The first claim has already been criticized above. The second was surely never very plausible, and has now been generally abandoned. There is clearly no correlation, for instance, between the numbers who support a particular campaign or demand and that campaign's influence and effectiveness – as there should be, to some extent, according to democratic principles. Nor is an organization's capacity to mobilize public support in meetings or demonstrations necessarily influential or even advantageous. On the contrary, it is clear that some pressure groups and their campaigns are successful because they are the expressions of existing economic power, because they are lavishly financed, and because they are supported by 'important' people rather than ordinary people. The successful campaign to introduce commercial television into Britain in the 1950s is a good example of this.[3] The decision to introduce a television channel financed by advertising was one which had to be taken by government. It was thus a political decision in the strictest sense, but it was taken not in response to any kind of popular pressure, but in response to a narrowly but powerfully based pressure-group campaign in which those who stood to gain most financially, such as the makers of television sets, played a prominent role. That commercial television then proved to be popular is beside the point. There was nothing democratic about either the way in which the decision was taken or the process which led up to it.

Inequality in wealth and economic power, in other words, is a form of political inequality, which contradicts the principle of political equality expressed in the slogan 'one person, one vote'. For example, the ownership and control of newspapers, television and radio stations and channels is, from one angle, simply a form of economic power, obtained by buying these commodities, like any other kind of private ownership. But it is perfectly clear that media ownership is also a form of political power, and it is used as such by the owners. To those who possess this kind of power to influence or even determine political outcomes, the possession of the single individual vote must seem by comparison a trivial and irrelevant form of political participation.

Other forms of inequality, social, racial and sexual, also run counter to the principle of political equality. No one with any

experience of political meetings or grass-roots political movements
and organizations can fail to have noticed how easily and naturally
such groups and gatherings are dominated by white, bourgeois,
educated males. The advantages and privileges attaching to class,
race and gender make it seem quite 'natural' that this should be so.
Even what are supposed to be working-class interests are often led
and dominated by the middle class, as has frequently been
observed. Whatever the effect on the parties concerned, this cannot
be healthy from a democratic point of view. Nor can the undoubted
fact that middle- or upper-class pressure groups and campaigns are
generally much more politically effective than attempts to mobilize
working-class interests. Nor can the often minimal presence of
women in the politics and elected assemblies of the Western
democracies. Ethnic minorities, too, are often strikingly under-
represented, in proportion to their numbers, in such assemblies.

Such discrepancies cannot be viewed as accidental or simply self-
chosen. They are an expression of underlying inequalities which,
while they may be categorized primarily as economic and social,
must also be seen as political. There is therefore a tension between
the continued existence of economic and social inequalities which
confer political advantages on some groups and corresponding
disadvantages on others, and the democratic principle of political
equality, which ought, as a principle, to mean not merely equality
in the voting booth but also equality of access to the political
decision-makers, and equal opportunities to influence the policies
and direction taken by society as a whole. As things stand, in most
modern representative democracies, the voting booth is the one
place and time at which we all have equal power – one person, one
vote. Every other form of power is most unevenly and unequally
distributed.

But we can go further than that. In classical political thinking,
'democracy' was the name not merely of a form of government but
of a whole society, and it was habitually associated, by its enemies
and critics as well as its friends, with the principle of social equality.
Tocqueville's *Democracy in America* is, as has been noted, essentially a study of American society, and one commentator has even
suggested that it might better have been called *Equality in
America*.[4] If we wish to revive that tradition, or if we are interested
in creating a fully democratic society, then there can be no doubt
that a more than narrowly political or formal equality must be one
of our goals.

# Representation and 'Direct' Democracy

We must now, however, retrace our steps to some extent. Our earlier discussion of unanimity and of majority rule was based, at least in part, on the assumption of direct personal participation by each citizen in decision-making; and although many examples have been used from the practice of existing states which claim to be democracies, we have not as yet considered the principles of representation, or any of the procedures and processes which might bring indirect democracy more closely into line with the original ideal of rule by the people.

Virtually everywhere today, democracy is taken to be synonymous with some kind of representative system. Hence the addition of the term 'direct' to what, until about 150 years ago, was everywhere known simply as 'democracy'. Today the unqualified term has been appropriated for a form of democracy which is, at best, indirect. As we saw, democrats like Paine originally put forward representation as a means of adapting the democratic principle to societies, such as the United States, which were too large to allow for personal participation by all their citizens. For them it was an expedient, almost a makeshift, and one that contained obvious dangers. It was thought desirable to set up safeguards that would prevent the representatives from arrogating to themselves the powers and authority that properly belonged to the people.

But representative assemblies of a kind, parliaments, had a history which went back many centuries before the modern revival of the idea of democracy, and these assemblies brought with them their own rather different concept of representation. It was classically articulated by Edmund Burke in his 'Speech to the Electors of Bristol' of 3 November, 1774. Burke unequivocally rejected any idea of a 'mandate' or 'instructions' from his constituents as to how he should vote or what line he should take on any particular issue as 'things utterly unknown to the laws of this land', reflecting a misconception of 'the whole order and tenor of our constitution'. He argued that 'Your representative owes you, not his industry only, but his judgement; and he betrays, instead of serving you, if he sacrifices it to your opinion'. He asserted that Parliament was 'not a *congress* of ambassadors from different and hostile interests . . . but . . . a *deliberative* assembly with *one* interest, that of the whole – where nor local purposes, nor local prejudices ought to guide, but the general good, resulting from the general reason of the whole'[1]; a contention which contains more than an echo of Rousseau, ironically, since Rousseau was adamant that the nation could not be represented in the way Burke implies.

This idea of the representative having a right, and even a duty, to exercise an independent judgement, with this independence being the core of what is held to distinguish a representative from a mere delegate, is a notion which has long survived Burke's formulation of it. British Members of Parliament invariably use it in their own defence when their opinions diverge from those of their constituency parties; and the Labour Party's introduction of compulsory reselection for sitting MPs before each general election was one of the catalysts of the split in the party which led to the formation of the Social Democratic Party in 1981. To the Social Democrats this represented an interference with the traditional independence of the people's elected representatives.

Whatever arguments there may be in favour of the independence of members of assemblies or parliaments, it is hard to see what they have to do with representation as it is commonly understood. A representative must surely represent, or speak for, some body of persons or opinion other than her- or himself. A representative chosen by the people of a particular constituency should presumably speak for that constituency. As the term is commonly used, a representative, as opposed to a delegate, is not mandated to speak or vote in particular ways; but it has always been a puzzle to me to understand in what ways such a person can then be said to represent, or speak for, those who sent him or her there.

One possible answer to this is that such a person is felt to be not only a representative but also representative as a person of those who chose her or him. This point was well made by Aneurin Bevan:

A representative person is one who will act in a given situation in much the same way as those he represents would act in that same situation. In short, he must be of their kind . . . Election is only one part of representation. It becomes full representation only if the elected person speaks with the authentic accents of those who elected him . . . he should share their values; that is, be in touch with their realities.[2]

This may be thought to give some substance to the notion of representation, which otherwise remains remarkably vague and undemanding in the Burkean version. Nevertheless, the Burkean idea has prevailed in Western democratic politics, rather than the radical democratic position of Paine and the Chartists. The result is that, outside the electoral process, the people, those who are represented, have strikingly little control over what their representatives actually do in their name. It is hard to resist the conclusion that the distinction between a representative and a delegate, although real enough, is posed in misleading terms. Leaving aside Bevan's conception of the 'true' representative, it is not clear in what sense a Burkean representative is a representative at all. A true representative is surely someone who is authorized to speak and act on behalf of those she or he represents, and who has been so authorized by them. A true representative, in other words, is a delegate, carrying a mandate and acting under instructions.

The principle of the mandate is still invoked, of course, but in relation to parties rather than individual representatives. A governing party is apt to claim that it has a mandate for doing something which it said it would do in its election manifesto, or which it simply said it would do some time before being elected. The most this can mean is that the people who voted for the party did so knowing that it was planning to do certain things, and that therefore these voters can be assumed to have consented to those plans. This assumption is quite illegitimate. It is quite likely that the voters are in fact ignorant of those plans. But even if that is held to be culpable ignorance, it cannot be assumed that if the voters did know of those plans or intentions they approved of them. It is possible, and indeed likely, that many of them voted for the party despite some of its specific plans and intentions, and opinion polls sometimes indicate that a majority of those who support a party or government do so while opposing one or more of its particular policies. Votes are cast for candidates and parties. There is no way of telling whether they are cast in support of any particular policy or not. A party is not mandated to carry out particular policies in the sense of the term 'mandate' used above, and as it is commonly understood. So whether we are considering the current practice of representation in relation to individual representatives, or in relation to parties and those who vote for them, it is clear that popular control and accountability are at best very weakly embodied in that practice. This is not accidental, since in the case of Britain the official doctrine is that sovereignty resides in Parliament, not with the people. Hence, even when a referendum takes place in Britain, Parliament takes care to make it clear that it is only a 'consultative' measure. Parliament is not bound to follow public opinion, however clearly it might be expressed.

Even if the practice of representation was more thoroughly democratic than it is, and every precaution was taken to guard against what Walt Whitman memorably termed 'the never-ending audacity of elected persons', there are still problems, from a democratic point of view, inherent in the very principle of representation. Given the uniqueness of each individual, and given the gradations and shadings of opinion found even among those who are in broad agreement on a particular issue, representation, even of one person by another, let alone of a group by a single person, must always be approximate and imperfect. As D.H. Lawrence asked indignantly, 'who can represent me? – I am myself. I don't intend anybody to represent me'.[3] This fundamental protest, voiced in an eloquent essay on 'Democracy', finds, I suspect, a widespread echo even among those who are less fiercely individualistic than was Lawrence.

This problem is greatly exacerbated if, in practice, it is only the majority, or even the largest single minority, within a group that is actually represented. We saw earlier that majority decision-making, even in the context of direct participatory democracy, poses the problem of how those who oppose the majority position and vote against it can be said to be governing themselves. And it was suggested that their participation in the decision-making process, coupled with scrupulous adherence to principles of openness and fairness in that process, may persuade them to accept decisions and policies with which they do not agree. But in a representative system, where the representative speaks and votes only on behalf of the majority of the group represented, the minority in that group is not represented in the decision-making process at all. At the extreme, if it turned out that one opinion was in a minority in every group or constituency mandating its one representative, then the gathering of representatives would be unanimous in its support for the other opinion, while the minority opinion would be entirely unrepresented, even though, in principle, it could be held by 49 per cent of those taking part in the mandating process. If it is accepted that representative or indirect democracy is at best an inadequate substitute for personal participation, and that everything possible should be done to ensure that the views and wishes of the people are represented as accurately as possible within such a system, it must surely follow that representation should be in proportion to the weight of opinion in the society itself. The general principle of proportional representation is surely a more democratic one than any system which tends to overrepresent majorities at the cost of underrepresenting minorities – if they are lucky enough to be represented at all.

There are various ways in which popular opinion can be represented with reasonable accuracy. One is for the representative not to vote as an individual, but to cast for each position or proposition the number of votes cast for it by those she or he is there to represent. Another is to have more than one representative for each group or constituency, the representatives being mandated as nearly as possible in proportion to the distribution of opinion among the represented. At the parliamentary level, multi-member constituencies are partly designed to achieve this. This is not the place to enter into a detailed discussion of different electoral systems and their advantages and disadvantages; but it should be noted that those who oppose the general principle of proportional representation do not usually do so in terms of arguments about democracy and representation, but more often stress the need for strong and stable government. This may well be considered to be an important factor, but, like other arguments for restricting popular influence or control over political systems and assemblies, it is not a democratic argument. And it is often an explicitly anti-democratic one.

Apart, then, from those for whom the virtue of representative democracy is precisely that it restricts and restrains popular power, and even, as in Britain, involves the vesting of sovereignty in the representative institutions rather than in the people themselves, the chief argument in defence of representative democracy has been an essentially pragmatic one: that it is the best that can be devised in the context of large societies where the citizens are too many and too scattered to be gathered together in one place. It is time to examine the validity of this argument. How impracticable *is* direct democracy?

First, we should ask whether popular participation requires that all should be gathered together at one time in one place. Is there any reason why the same debate, or a debate on the same question, should not be conducted at more or less the same time in a great number of different places? Modern means of communication, particularly television, could easily overcome, if it were thought desirable, the isolation of any particular local assembly. 'Keynote' speeches or other important contributions to the debate could easily be relayed nationally. It would even be possible for people to watch a political or parliamentary debate at home on television, and then register their vote or opinion at the end of it by pressing a button or making a free telephone call. Of course, watching or half-watching a debate is not the same thing as taking part in one, and it might well be argued that that level or style of participation does not demand enough of the individual citizen. My point here is a simple one: modern technology has made the direct participation of the people in political debate and decision-making a perfectly practicable possibility.[4] Whether it is deemed desirable or not is a different question.

The referendum or plebiscite is a device viewed with suspicion in some quarters, largely because they have often been used to ratify or endorse decisions already taken or policies already embarked on, as was the case with Britain's entry into the European Economic Community, or because they have been staged, and the issue presented, in such a way as to produce the outcome wanted by the government which initiates them. They have, in other words, been gestures in the direction of popular consultation rather than anything more substantial, with governments often declining to accept their outcome as binding in any case. Thus referenda can be devalued, and they can be abused. But we should not conclude from this that they are therefore intrinsically objectionable and unworkable. On the contrary: once again it is hard to see what *democratic* objection there can be to the principle of allowing the people themselves to decide on major issues of principle. The two questions on which referenda were held in Britain in the 1970s, joining the EEC and creating some limited self-government in Scotland and Wales, are good examples of just such issues. It was significant that the devolution of some government to Scotland and Wales in 1998 did not go ahead until further referenda had been held to ascertain the degree of popular support for such changes. And it was striking that the referenda did stimulate a serious and extensive debate about the matters which were to be decided on.

If we move away from the national level to consider smaller local communities, or particular institutions such as factories and offices, colleges and schools, it is quite clear that there are no problems of either size or communications which stand in the way of their being governed according to the principle of direct participatory democracy. There may well be – there always are – other grounds for resisting the implementation of such a principle: it would be time-consuming, it would be costly, it would not work well, and so on. But the idea is certainly not impracticable. In fact the numbers involved at such levels would normally be far below the size of the citizen population of fifth-century BC Athens. One set of institutions in Britain which does practise direct democracy to some extent is that of student unions, which are governed in part by general meetings which all students are entitled to attend. Usually, of course, only a small proportion of the students do actually attend. Nevertheless, the principle is established that all students can participate in the decision-making process, and it is not a principle which has proved to be unworkable or which has produced manifestly absurd results. If people are seriously interested in extending the application of the democratic principle within our society, it is certainly a model that could be adopted and adapted without serious practical difficulties in many other institutions.

Within a short space I have been concerned to make two basic points in this chapter. The first is that even if we concluded that a representative democracy was the best that could be achieved under modern circumstances, the idea or principle of representation is far from being fully or effectively embodied in existing political arrangements. The second is that, in fact, direct democracy could be a great deal more widely practised than it actually is, and that some modern technological developments have made it easier to implement than it might have been a century ago. If, despite that, there is very little direct democracy in most contemporary societies, the reasons for that are political rather than practical or technical: those who occupy positions of power and authority simply do not want it, and actively resist any attempt to bring it into being. Opposition to democracy is not as moribund as public rhetoric might lead us to suppose.

# Consent, Freedom
# and Debate

Just as democracy is sometimes loosely equated with majority rule, so at others it has been identified with government by consent. As was suggested earlier, there are good reasons for not identifying democracy solely with a system of government; nevertheless, we must look a little more closely at the notion of consent. For an alternative formulation might be that the hallmark of democratic government (which is not the whole of democracy) is government by consent, by contrast with other forms of arbitrary or tyrannical rule where the wishes of the people are ignored and their assent or support is not sought or considered necessary.

There are two problems with this line of argument. The first is that it need not be democratic government, or democratic propositions, to which the people give their consent. That suspicion of the referendum or plebiscite which we noted in the previous chapter was partly based on the fact that it is a device which had been used by some dictators and despots to give their rule at least the semblance of a basis in popular consent. The pioneer in this respect was Emperor Napoleon III in the 1850s. But whatever the degree of manipulation involved in specific instances, it is clearly possible in principle for genuine popular consent and active support to be given to a dictatorship or to an authoritarian regime, as it was given by the Germans to Hitler in the early 1930s, or to specific measures intended to restrict or even destroy democracy. It is conceivable that the people can consent to the abolition of democracy. If consent is the essence of democracy, we would have to accept that that could be a democratic act.

This is the impasse into which the equation of democracy with consent can lead us. It is pointless to deny that a dictatorship *can* rest on popular support, or that under certain circumstances a majority of the people can be persuaded to support or endorse illib- eral and anti-democratic policies. The phenomenon of popular authoritarianism is not altogether the invention of frightened bour- geois liberals. But if we now recall the alternative definition of democracy as popular power, or popular sovereignty, then clearly it cannot be a *democratic* act for the people to vote away their own power and their own rights, any more than if I freely renounce my freedom I can remain free because the renunciation was a free act. For democracy to exist, power must remain with the people. If they freely abdicate that power, what they consent to may have popular support, but it is not democracy. This argument is analogous to, though not identical with, Rousseau's contention that sovereignty belongs to the people and cannot be transferred by them to any other body or person. To talk about 'inalienable sovereignty' has a somewhat old-fashioned metaphysical air about it nowadays. Nevertheless, Paine makes much the same point as Rousseau in his contention, in *Rights of Man*, that:

> Every age and generation must be as free to act for itself, in all cases, as the ages and generations which preceded it . . . Man has no property in man; neither has any generation a property in the generations which are to follow.[1]

If every generation has the right to decide for itself how it should be governed, then it cannot be legitimate for one generation to will away that right on behalf of its successors. One generation may sign away democracy, or consent to dictatorship, but the next has an absolute right to revoke those decisions. So, in effect, popular sovereignty must be inalienable if it is to mean anything at all substantial.

The other problem with the concept of consent is simply that it is susceptible of very weak and even negative interpretations. Even authoritarian regimes, if they are to last, must be able to count on some measure of consent, though not necessarily that of a major- ity. Brute force, however effective in terrorizing people, is not by itself enough in the longer run. Consent in such circumstances does not have to be formally registered: it is enough for the regime that it can count, in practice, on the support and co-operation of key sectors of the population. It is tempting for any regime to claim that its very survival proves that it has consent and support. And such a claim might be based on the notion of 'tacit consent'. Tacit consent

was the tactic which Locke used in his *Second Treatise* to escape
from the dilemma of reconciling his basic principle – 'The *Liberty
of Man*, in Society, is to be under no other Legislative Power, but
that established, by consent, in the Commonwealth' (22, p. 301) –
with the desirability of a stable and durable system of government
which would not have to be submitted to the people for constant
re-endorsement. People were deemed to consent to the system of
government they were born under when they came of age by virtue
of the fact of their remaining within that particular society. The lack
of positive objection was interpreted as consent. Unless you with-
drew from the society, you were deemed to have contracted into it
(see 119, p. 366).

Silence means consent. In practice, and at innumerable levels
where decisions have to be made, this assumption is made all the
time. Perhaps it has to be. It is nevertheless a false equation, and at
times a seriously misleading one. The negative failure to object, or
to opt out, may signify one of a whole range of reactions: fear or
prudence in the face of power, indifference, paralysis of the will,
sullen resignation, sheer hopelessness, a feeling of ignorance, or
habits of subservience. Any or all of these may lie submerged
beneath a surface of silence. They clearly are not identical with
consent. But the facile equation of silence with consent frequently
results in those in power forming exaggerated ideas of the degree
of support or acquiescence they can command. They are then dis-
agreeably surprised when the resentments and even despair which
are so often concealed by silence break out in angry and violent
rebellion.

Never was this more dramatically demonstrated than by the collapse of the Communist regimes of eastern Europe in and around
the year 1989. The passivity, the silence, the acquiescence of the
peoples of East Germany, Czechoslovakia and Hungary in previous
years must have tempted the rulers of those countries to believe
that, even if they were not exactly popular, then at least their rule
was accepted, and in that sense consented to. They must have been
astounded by the uprisings of the autumn of 1989; yet the very
swiftness with which the *anciens régimes* of Communism crumbled
demonstrated their ultimate hollowness, the lack of genuine and
positive support for them. The 'silence' of most of Czechoslovakia
in the twenty years between the crushing of the Prague Spring in
1968 and the popular uprising of 1989 indicated not any kind of
consent, but resignation, hopelessness and despair, all reinforced

by the fear inspired by the regime's relentless persecution of those who dared to oppose it.

But even when consent is given a more positive content, and a definite 'yes' is required rather than the mere absence of 'no', it remains an indelibly passive concept. Consent is essentially a response to initiatives taken by someone else. The initiative still lies with governments, parties, political leaders. But why should the people's role be so confined? A.D. Lindsay asked the relevant question over seventy years ago:

> Is democracy a means of bringing about that the people shall consent to what the government proposes to do, or that the government shall do what the people want? The two things are very different, and yet if all we want is to produce consent, it can be got in either way.[2]

Consent, then, is too passive and restrictive a conception to provide an adequate account of the proper role of the people in a democracy. But how are they to play a more positive role? Is it realistic to expect initiatives to come from the people themselves? For that to be possible there are certain conditions, not so far discussed, which must be fulfilled.

First, there must be a climate of freedom within which opinions can be freely expressed and discussion conducted without fear or restraint. Democracy requires freedom. It has been one of the clichés of modern liberalism, since at least the time of Tocqueville and the younger Mill, to dwell on the possible, even probable, disjunction between democracy and liberty, to stress the fact that popular rule does not necessarily imply personal freedom, and to conjure up the spectacle of the 'tyranny of the majority'. It is certainly true that popular rule, considered in the simplest terms, does not logically imply a commitment to respect individual liberty: there can be such a thing as popular tyranny, or a popularly endorsed tyranny. And there clearly are situations in which the collective opinion of a majority or even a dominant minority puts an unacceptable and sometimes intolerable pressure on the dissenting or deviant minority or individual.

Against this liberal orthodoxy it is worth making two points. The first is that there is rather little reason to associate the coercive pressure of a dominant or majority current of opinion or belief with democracy. Closed societies, marked by a high degree of coherence in belief and custom, can be found throughout history. They are often, and perhaps even typically, characterized by authoritarian rather than democratic forms of government. Unless collective pressure is to be treated as democratic by definition, the only ground for especially associating it with democracy is that democracy might be held to give collective pressure an exceptional legitimacy. But this is so only if we equate democracy with a simple and unrestrained majoritarianism, and, as we have seen, there are good democratic reasons for not making that equation.

Second, it is very striking that this liberal disjunction between liberty and democracy so readily overlooks the fact that in history the struggle for democracy and the struggle for fundamental liberties have very often been one and the same. The British radicals, including the Chartists, who campaigned for a democratic franchise in the early nineteenth century, also campaigned for a free press, by which they meant one unhampered by government censorship and taxes. This was by no means fortuitous. How could the working class make effective use of the political power which the vote was expected to give them without the opportunity to engage in an open discussion of political principle and perspectives? Or, more widely, how could citizens fulfil their role in a democracy without undergoing some political education, and how was such an education possible without free communications and free debate?

The assumption that there is a necessary connection between democracy and freedom is surely correct, even if we take some of the narrower definitions of democracy. For example, even if the essence of democracy is taken to be the process of choosing between elites competing to govern, the very business of choosing can hardly be confined to the visit to the polling booth. The parties (or elites) must be allowed to publish their programmes and make their competing claims to office; the elector must be able to question them, and voice his or her doubts or support. Once public debate is permitted in the election period, prohibiting it at other times becomes difficult. Choice, however limited in scope, implies debate, and debate implies a degree of freedom, even if limits are set on what can be debated.

If we adopt the more expansive conception of democracy which has been used throughout this book, the case is even stronger. Democracy as popular power, it has been suggested, should be seen as a continuous process of interaction between government and society, with a maximum involvement of the people in public decision-making at every level. A parody of this, a pseudo-democracy, occurs when the decision-makers put on a show of consulting those whom their decisions affect when in fact the crucial decisions have already been taken and the policies decided on. These are the circumstances in which, as Lindsay shrewdly observed, 'consent can be manufactured' (p. 43). If, however, genuine, convinced, voluntary consent is being sought, then free and open discussion cannot be avoided, for what genuine consent needs is that people should feel quite free to voice their doubts and opposition, if only to create the possibility of overcoming such doubts and hostility. And if we look to the people to play a more positive role, freely voicing their demands and hopes, their fears and grievances, as well as introducing ideas and initiating policies, plainly this can only happen in an atmosphere of the greatest possible freedom and openness, free from any taint of intimidatory anxiety or apprehension as to the possible consequences of speaking out.

That individuals and groups should feel free and unintimidated is certainly a necessary condition of free discussion, free decision-making and free consent; but it is not a sufficient condition. People may possibly *feel* free and independent even when they are actually being manipulated. What seems to the individual to be a free and spontaneous response can be seen from 'outside' to be the product of either social and ideological conditioning or, in some cases, of a concerted campaign to mould public opinion. This can produce a response which each individual feels and believes to be authentically his or hers alone. As Hans Magnus Enzensberger observed in a notable essay on 'The Industrialization of the Mind':

> All of us, no matter how irresolute we are, like to think that we reign supreme in our own consciousness, that we are masters of what our minds accept or reject ... No illusion is more stubbornly upheld than the sovereignty of the mind.

And yet, since at least the time of Hegel and Marx, we have been increasingly aware that, as Enzensberger's paraphrase of Marx has it, 'What is going on in our minds has always been, and will always be a product of society'.[3] There is a history of ideas, and it is the history both of how human beings shape ideas and of how ideas shape human beings. The idea that the individual's mind can remain a wholly independent entity, uninfluenced by its social and intellectual environment, is certainly a piece of individualist mythology. On the other hand, we cannot say that people are making up their minds for themselves so long as they are largely unaware of the influences that are playing upon them, and so long as those influences are not essentially diverse and competitive, but generally combine to push their thinking, their attitudes and feelings in a single direction.

Free debate, free choice and genuine consent require, then, a level of education (which may not be a formal education) in social understanding such that people are aware of themselves as the targets of persuasion and propaganda, and are thereby enabled to resist these pressures. But it also requires a distribution of the resources for propaganda and persuasion which ensures that the power to influence our minds is distributed roughly in accord with the degree of diversity of opinion within society. If people are exposed to the normal variety of opinions around any major issue, the likelihood of their easy manipulation by unscrupulous opinion-makers is greatly reduced. Contrary to what some ideologues would have us believe, this diversity is not spontaneously produced by the operations of the market. Look at the current pattern of ownership of the press, television and radio outside public-sector broadcasting. In Britain, at least, communications are dominated by a few millionaire proprietors and a few large conglomerate companies. Consequently there is not a single national daily or Sunday newspaper which consistently supports any political position further left than 'New' Labour, while the majority of newspapers purvey a range of typically Right-wing attitudes which extend far beyond the relatively narrow confines of purely party politics.

There is, of course, nothing surprising about this. Millionaires are unlikely to be social or political radicals. But so long as millionaires, or their corporate equivalents, are the only ones who can readily own newspapers or television companies, it is certain that the media will not accurately reflect either the range or the balance of opinions, ideas and beliefs within society, and consequently that there cannot be a properly balanced and open debate on political issues within society.

A popular participatory democracy is a system in which decisions are taken, and policies made, as a result of the widest possible free and open discussion. As Lindsay puts it:

> In a healthy democracy the discussions of the representative assembly will as it were act as chairman for the multifarious informal discussion of the nation as a whole, and the measure of the successful working of

democracy is the extent to which the voting of the ordinary man and woman has been informed by this widely diffused public discussion. (p. 42)

Not only should government consult people about what it proposes to do. The health of democracy requires that government should be not merely ready, but obliged, to listen to what the people (in all their multiplicity) have to say. Leaders and government have to be accessible to the people; and, given the great gulf between them in so many modern societies, this probably means that the government has to go to the people, rather than expecting the people to come to it. In this respect it looks as if some Latin American leaders and regimes have understood better what is needed than the more formal and even ossified democracies of the West. So Salman Rushdie, visiting Nicaragua in 1986, noted of President Daniel Ortega that:

> Talking to the people was a priority for his administration. He regularly took his entire cabinet to meet the people in popular forums, making himself accountable in a way his main western critics never would. I tried to imagine Ronald Reagan or Margaret Thatcher agreeing to submit themselves to a monthly grilling by members of the public, and failed.[4]

Graham Greene, in Panama a few years earlier, noticed a similar style of popular consultation and accessibility being used by General Omar Torrijos and his government, and suggested that the country 'had evolved a very different form of democracy' from Britain's, but one with its own validity.[5]

Nor was this an isolated observation on Greene's part. Visiting Cuba in the early post-revolutionary years, in 1963, Greene noted: 'There is a touch of ancient Athens about Havana today; the Republic is small enough for the people to meet in the *agora*.' And at that time Fidel Castro, like Omar Torrijos, seemed extraordinarily accessible to those Cubans who wanted to see him – 'more accessible than Mr Macmillan', wrote Greene.[6]

Accessibility and a readiness to listen are not, to be sure, incompatible with a fundamentally authoritarian structure of power and government. Nor is making a show of consultation and participation, when what is being looked for is essentially a ratification of decisions already taken. This is the appearance of democracy without the substance. The substance is the power of the people to make governments, and make their representatives, accede to the popular will and to popular demands. Democracy involves debate and discussion, but these are not enough if they remain inconclusive and ineffective in determining actual policies. It is at this point that the concept of 'deliberative democracy' becomes important. Democracy is conceived not simply in terms of who decides, but also as the process through which decisions and policies are made. That process is participatory, and policies are not simply proposed and debated, but are evolved through discussion, and by taking into account, as far as possible, the variety of interests and viewpoints expressed by those involved in the debate. The outcome of such discussions should be popular decisions and popular demands; and since in a democracy it is the people, and not the government or parliament, who are sovereign, it is then the business of government to accept and to implement the popular will.

# 10
# Conclusion: Creating Democracy

If the interpretation of democracy argued for in this book is correct, or at least is found persuasive by its readers, then clearly the principal practical implication is that democracy is still 'unfinished business' on the agenda of modern politics – and not only for those polities which are, as it were, 'officially' recognized to be in the process of being democratized. Even when universal suffrage is achieved, or when popular election becomes a central part of the political system, democracy is far from being fully realized. Those two very substantial and important achievements might reasonably be regarded as only the first steps on the road to the creation of a fully democratic society. The fact that Russians now elect their president, to take one example, can hardly be said to make post-Communist Russia a democracy. Given the power of the presidency, the weakness of the parliament, and the degree of control which the government exercises over the press and broadcasting, it would be more accurate to describe Russia as being governed by an 'elected dictatorship'.

In the West we have inherited from the Cold War the lazy assumption that if a country's government is not Communist, or is not that of an identifiable dictator, then it must be a democracy. But one purpose of this book has been to argue for a more strict and demanding conception of democracy than that implied by such casual beliefs. Occasional more or less free elections are not in themselves enough to pass the democratic 'test'.

This is not, however, to suggest that popular election is negligible or unimportant. There is, or was, a kind of crude and debased variant of Marxism which tended to regard the differences in political systems and state structures among capitalist societies as fundamentally superficial and unimportant. Bourgeois democracy was seen as a façade, behind which the capitalist class continued to rule and dominate bourgeois society. Consequently, it mattered little whether the façade was retained or stripped away to reveal the reality behind. Indeed the latter might be preferable, since it would leave the class enemy clearly in view. This was the way in which some Communists reacted to the advent of Nazism in 1933. It proved to be an exceptionally costly misjudgement. What were once thought of as 'mere' political 'forms' are now recognized to be of far greater potential and actual importance than an exclusive concentration on economic and social power might suggest.

Any tendency, therefore, to undervalue the virtues, advantages and opportunities afforded by 'bourgeois' democracy ought to be firmly resisted. It is an achievement to be built on rather than despised or disregarded. This is likely to be most deeply appreciated in countries which until recently have either never known it, such as South Africa or Poland, or have recovered it with difficulty, such as Chile and the Czech Republic. Nevertheless, 'bourgeois' democracy has proved in more than one respect to be a false dawn, realizing only a part of the promise sought by so many of those who struggled to achieve it. In Britain, for example, the first Reform Act of 1832 was preceded by decades of intermittent popular struggle, in which leading figures like William Cobbett argued ceaselessly against insurrectionary designs and in favour of channelling popular radicalism towards the strictly constitutional objective of a wider franchise. There is no doubt that the outcome of that long campaign, the Act itself, was a bitter disappointment to working-class radicals. As Cobbett said afterwards, the people had wanted the Act 'that it might do us some good; that it might better our situation . . . and not for the gratification of any abstract or metaphysical whim.'[1] The same was true of the Chartists. They saw universal, or manhood, suffrage not so much as an end in itself as the key which would unlock the door to radical or even revolutionary social and economic change. Their class opponents shared that expectation, and feared and fought the extension of the franchise for that reason. The subsequent reconciliation of the bourgeoisie to 'the coming of democracy' owed much to the fact that these fears (or hopes) were not realized, or realized at best only in part. A similar comment can be made on the fierce struggle for women's suffrage in Britain in the early part of the twentieth century. Like Cobbett, many suffragettes would have said that it was not so much the vote for its own sake that they sought as the improvements in the status and conditions of women which they believe would be achieved as the result of women's enfranchisement. It would be foolish to suggest that getting the vote had no beneficial consequences for women. On the other hand, the revival of the women's movement since the 1960s bears witness to the failure of women's suffrage in itself to achieve substantive equality between the sexes, or even to abolish some of the more blatant forms of discrimination against women enshrined in much traditional law and practice.

There are signs today of a similar disenchantment in eastern Europe and the former Soviet Union. It is not that people do not value their hard-won, long-denied freedoms, where these have been achieved. Nor do most of them yearn for the 'good old days' of authoritarianism and government by party decree. But, as in nineteenth-century Britain or revolutionary France, the mass of the people expect and want democracy to 'do us some good'; and the present combination of democracy with capitalism is not producing better material conditions for the mass of the people than did authoritarian Communism. Indeed, the imposition from above of 'free market' principles has created much misery and hardship. Gavriil Popov, elected mayor of Moscow in 1990, wrote with unusual candour about the conflict between popular aspirations and what he and other political leaders deemed to be the necessary transformation of the economy:

> But now we must create a society with a variety of different forms of ownership, including private property; and this will be a society of economic inequality . . . [But] the masses long for fairness and economic equality. And the further the process of transformation goes, the more acute and the more glaring will be the gap between those aspirations and economic realities.[2]

Popov and other eastern European 'reformers', along with many of their most enthusiastic Western supporters, would no doubt indignantly deny the suggestion that there might be some inherent and ineradicable tensions, or even contradictions, between democracy and capitalism, with its casual acceptance of unlimited economic inequalities. Nevertheless, that is one way in which his own statement could be read.

So we must at least conclude from this that the purposes for which ordinary people wanted political democracy, or the vote, have not yet been completely fulfilled by any means. But it has been argued here that we should go further than that, and recognize that political democracy itself has not been realized simply by giving every adult person a vote in general and local elections. The principle of equality of political power, which is embodied in the possession by each and every citizen of one vote, stands in sharp contrast to the blatant inequalities in the distribution of political power in almost every other important respect. This is not just a matter of looking at the distribution of power and influence in relation to official decision-making bodies, or even of power over the minds and feelings of the people themselves, although in both cases that distribution is manifestly and grotesquely uneven. It is also a question of understanding power itself, how it is exerted and where it lies. To illustrate what is meant, here is an example. In his valuable and revealing *Diaries of a Cabinet Minister* R.H.S. Crossman gave an account of how the Labour Cabinet of which he was a member in the 1960s had to decide whether to allow an oil company to build a refinery on Canvey Island in Essex. Not surprisingly, the proposal was strongly opposed by many residents of the area, and Crossman, as Minister for Housing, had some sympathy with them. But when the issue came before the Cabinet it decided in favour of the oil company: 'The Foreign Office, the Commonwealth Office, the Ministry of Power, the D.E.A. [Department of Economic Affairs] and the Treasury all insisted that we couldn't afford to upset a foreign oil company.'[3] The risks involved in displeasing the company were deemed to be too great. Against that local opposition counted for very little.

Here is an example of a political decision being taken more than 30 years ago at the highest level by an elected government which nevertheless felt itself to be more or less powerless in relation to a large transnational company. It is clear that the power of the company is political as well as economic. But unlike the local community, which would have had to organize, collect signatures for a petition, demonstrate and lobby in order to make its views heard and get them noticed, the company needed to *do* very little. Certainly it had no need to solicit public support. Provided that the Cabinet was aware of the company's power, which of course it was, the company had little need to campaign or lobby for its case. Its mere possession of power was enough to overawe the Cabinet into acceding to its 'request'. So not only the visible and active exercise of power needs to be equalized, but also the possession of power, which, where it cannot be redistributed, must at least be made accountable within the framework of democracy. The distinction between political and economic power, however useful as an analytical tool in certain circumstances, is fundamentally artificial. Economic power is political power, and it makes no sense to implement the principle of equality in respect of votes while leaving every other form of political power to be distributed according to the gross inequities of the capitalist market, even though this is overwhelmingly the prevailing pattern in the post-Communist world in which capital is so strongly in the ascendant.

There is thus, I would argue, a logic in the principle of democracy which points towards socialism. That elected governments find it necessary to bow to the wishes of big privately owned companies, that the media which so largely shape public opinion can be bought and sold by millionaires and treated by them simply as pieces of private property (which is, of course, what they are), demonstrates how difficult it is for an active and effective democracy to coexist with monopoly capitalism.

This conflict between the power of elected governments, accountable to the people and elected to pursue and promote the general good, and the power of privately owned and controlled corporate giants, accountable, if at all, only to their shareholders, and even then often only nominally so, grows more acute day by day and year by year. It is going to provide perhaps the most important test of the strength and vitality of democracy in the twenty-first century:

> The struggle between people and corporations will be the defining battle of the twenty-first century. If the corporations win, liberal democracy will come to an end. The great social democratic institutions which have defended the weak against the strong – equality before the law, representative government, democratic accountability, and the sovereignty of parliament – will be toppled. If, on the other hand, the corporate attempt on public life is beaten back, then democracy may re-emerge the stronger for its conquest.[4]

George Monbiot's prophecy may seem rather apocalyptic, but it is not only a struggle for power which is involved: what is at stake is the legitimacy of elected governments, and hence of democracy itself. A system of government that is perceived to be ineffectual or powerless loses public respect and confidence, and that can prepare the way for its overthrow or collapse. Democracy is replaced, perhaps gradually rather than abruptly, by some form of authoritarianism, and authoritarianism is accepted because it is seen to be effective. (Supposedly, it makes the trains run on time.)

This is why the decline in participation in elections, most marked in the United States, but noticeable also in Britain, where the percentage voting in the 2001 general election fell below 60 for the first time since universal adult suffrage was introduced in 1928, is a worrying phenomenon. Politicians tend to ascribe this to 'voter apathy', which they naturally deplore. But it may just as well reflect a widespread belief that 'voting does not change anything', that changes of government are unimportant because real power lies outside the control of government. In so far as this perception is correct, non-voting is not so clearly irrational as it would be if it were the product of laziness and irresponsibility. And it will take more than exhortations to reverse the trend.

The imbalance of power between governments and private corporations and companies, which, as we have seen, was apparent even in the 1960s, has grown dramatically in the past three decades, not least because governments themselves have encouraged and abetted it. The pros and cons of privatization as an economic strategy are obviously a matter of debate. But what can hardly be denied is that the privatization of so many functions and properties which were previously in the public sector, and for which, therefore, government was ultimately responsible, represents a substantial shift of power away from government into the private sector. This process may have been initiated by the conservative governments of the 1980s, led by Margaret Thatcher in Britain and Ronald Reagan in the United States. But it has been very widely taken up by governments of all political shades, including the Labour governments in Britain after 1997.

These developments have sometimes been defended by the politicians and their supporters with claims that the era of 'big government' is over. It is time to devolve power downwards into 'civil society'. This sounds like a process of democratization, and it would obviously be welcome if it were so. The devolution of powers within Britain to the Welsh Assembly and the Scottish Parliament is certainly a move which brings government closer to the people it is meant to serve and represent. But devolved government is the exception which confirms the general rule. The powers of which central government has more or less voluntarily divested itself are seldom transferred to elected and accountable public authorities.

In Britain the powers and responsibilities of elected local government have been steadily restricted and diminished rather than
expanded. 'Civil society' is a seductive phrase, but it often acts as
an attractive umbrella beneath which lurk oligopolies and concen-
trations of unaccountable power, whose relation with the rest of
society is one of domination, not collaboration.

Another response of government has been to talk the language
of 'partnership'. If, for example, private companies are allowed to
own and run schools, prisons or hospitals, which nevertheless
remain in principle public institutions, that is called a 'public–
private partnership'. The implication is that this is a relationship
between equals, but that is, of course, the issue that is in question.
How far is the public interest, or the general good, being compro-
mised or sacrificed to the narrower, commercial interests of the
companies to which control over these institutions has been given?

The record so far is not particularly reassuring. When, for
example, companies start supplying 'learning packs' to schools,
they naturally take the opportunity to promote the products they
sell, and to discredit criticism of or opposition to those products and
the processes they use – such as the environmental damage which
may be involved. This is only to be expected. 'The kids we're reaching', said one marketing manager, 'are consumers in training'. Such
attitudes subvert the independence and honesty of education. We
learn, too, that the Private Finance Initiative, under which new
hospitals are being built in Britain, can mean that the location of a
hospital is determined not by its convenience to patients but by the
profitability of the site; and that the payment of fees and debts to
the private company involved takes priority over the actual
spending on health provision.[5]

For the politicians, this devolution or transfer of power and
responsibility to private companies has an obvious appeal. They
can disown any responsibility for what is then done. Contemporary
governments, for instance, disclaim any intention of intervening in
industrial or wage disputes between workers and employers. These
two 'private' groups or bodies must settle matters themselves. But
such disputes, like the activities of 'private' companies which
control schools, hospitals and prisons, usually have many public
repercussions. And although politicians have been busy trying to
educate the public into expecting much less of government and the
state than they have been used to over the past half century and
more, they have not been especially successful. The public persists

in expecting the governments they elect to 'do something' about public problems and crises. Like the nineteenth-century campaigners for parliamentary reform, they expect elected government to 'do us some good'. Inactivity, hand wringing and shoulder shrugging do not much impress them.

If real power lay in the hands of ordinary people, and the organizations and campaigns they generate, popular expectations of government might be different, and more modest. The incentive to self-help would be far greater, and politicians' exhortations to practise it far more effective, if it yielded substantial results. But, as the residents of Canvey Island and Bedfordshire (see Chapter 6), along with countless thousands of others, discovered, popular opinion counts for little when weighed against the interests and influences of economically powerful companies and industries. And, at the time of writing (2002), the present British (Labour) government is proposing to make planning processes even more amenable to the convenience of the big companies, and even less open to effective local popular opposition.

There is no inevitable historical process which guarantees a slow but steady advance in the direction of a fuller and more effective democracy. The degree of democracy that has been achieved globally is still quite limited, and, even where it seems securely established, it is, in many ways, precarious and insecure. Under such rubrics as the need to guard against 'terrorism', individual rights, including the right to demonstrate and protest, are eaten away by governments with an inclination towards authoritarianism. And at the same time the power and acknowledged responsibilities of elected governments are being allowed to shrink in relation to the ever-growing power of vast transnational corporations, some of which now conduct a volume of economic activity greater than that of many small and relatively poor nation-states. Such corporations now tower threateningly over elected governments like giants in a child's nightmare. But this is no nightmare, but daily reality.

What is most disturbing is that this shrinkage in the scope and responsibility of elected, accountable government is not being resisted by most democratic governments themselves. On the contrary, they seem to have abandoned the old struggle to defend the general good against the narrow particular interests of private agglomerations of power; and some have even suggested that the general good is to be identified with those particular interests. With the often enthusiastic support of many Western governments, the presence and power of the great corporations in our public life are increasing all the time. Sometimes the forms of this presence (sponsorship, logos) seem harmless enough. But they display, for all to see, the increased dependency of the relatively powerless, who include elected local authorities, on the power and munificence of these rich, self-serving companies and enterprises. These are not democratic developments; they are anti-democratic developments. And they suggest that the complacency and even triumphalism which followed the collapse of European Communism, and assorted other dictatorships, around 1990, was badly misplaced. We are not necessarily progressing towards greater democracy, greater public and popular control of power; we may be moving away from it.

The growth of non-accountable corporate power over public life creates a lack of popular confidence in democracy itself which can only be rectified by bringing more and more of that power into the public and accountable sector. By the public sector I do not mean primarily the state; I mean a system of popular control within which producers and users (or consumers) would, as appropriate, share in policy- and decision-making. For it is one of the most noticeable features of the 'actually existing democracies' (to adapt a useful phrase of Rudolf Bahro's) that the democratic principle is confined to a very few public institutions and many voluntary organizations, while a vast range of centrally important institutions continue to be run by largely unaccountable and unelected oligarchies and individual autocrats. If we are interested in creating a democratic *society* there is clearly a great deal of work yet to be done.

And it would be foolish to imagine that the Western democracies have a monopoly of the relevant experience in that respect. Reference was made, in the previous chapter, to the patterns of dialogue between leaders and people practised in some of the more radical countries of Latin America. Significantly, too, in the final years of the Soviet Union, its last leader, Mikhail Gorbachev, was particularly concerned to introduce the principle of democracy into the area of work and production:

> The development of democracy in production is of paramount significance ... The economy is the decisive area of society's life. Tens of millions of people are occupied there daily. Therefore the development of democracy in production is the most important trend in deepening and broadening socialist democracy as a whole.[6]

It was later reported that Soviet television covered the election of a factory director by delegates representing the workforce of 13,000.[7] How far this pattern was followed, and how open was the choice of candidates, it is hard now to discover. But it is relevant to the present argument to note that this is a dimension of democracy which has been very little practised, or even discussed, in the officially democratic West, and which certainly does not feature within the recently privatized enterprises of Russia and eastern Europe. And yet, as Raymond Williams has written, 'It is difficult to feel that we are really governing ourselves if in so central a part of our living as our work most of us have no share in decisions that immediately affect us'.[8] Democracy in industry, or, more broadly, at the work place, is an idea that has often been discussed, but with a few exceptions (including the former Yugoslavia to some extent) has hardly as yet been embarked on as a serious practice in most societies.

Even if we adopt a much narrower focus and look at the specific-ally political institutions of the proclaimed democracies, it is plain that there is a long way to go before democratic principles are fully embodied in them. Britain is probably unique among democracies in retaining so many pre-democratic principles and institutions in a professedly democratic context. In Britain an elected chamber of Parliament coexists with one that is wholly non-elected and con-sists, at the time of writing, of a few descendants of a hereditary feudal aristocracy together with a majority composed of the beneficiaries of the patronage of successive prime ministers. It is not clear that the reformed House of Lords which is due to come into existence in the next few years will be clearly more democratic than the present half-way house. The principle of popular sover-eignty has never been accepted in Britain: instead sovereignty is shared between Parliament and a hereditary monarch. The principle of fixed-date elections has never been established: instead choosing the date of the general election remains one of the vast range of powers of patronage and manipulation in the hands of the incumbent prime minister. The electoral system itself, which favours first and second parties, increasingly produces a distri-bution of seats in the House of Commons which is sharply at vari-ance with the actual pattern of votes cast.

These are only the most obvious undemocratic anomalies within the British political system. It is a welcome and encouraging development that in recent years these anomalies and anachronisms

have attracted a good deal of criticism. Charter 88 and other groupings have done much to focus attention on how much remains to be
done before Britain can call itself a fully liberal democracy – to say
nothing of any more radical developments. But beyond these
specific reforms lies a more troubling general question. The British
Parliament itself, like some others, is in fact a pre-democratic and
pre-modern institution, as is manifest from its anachronistic construction, customs, language and overall ethos. The question is
whether these hallowed archaisms are only a surface phenomenon
which a sensible modernization of Parliament would easily sweep
away, or whether they suggest that the traditional kind of representative institution cannot cope with the problems of modern democratic government. This is not a new anxiety. It lurked in the pages
of Lindsay's *Essentials of Democracy*, published back in 1929, and
it was raised from a slightly different angle a few years later by
Harold Laski, when he asked 'whether political democracy has not,
so to say, arrived too late upon the scene to control the total process
by which it is confronted'.[9] Writing in the mid-1930s, he was thinking of the huge growth in the power of banks and oligopolies which
seemed beyond the capacity of Parliament to comprehend or to
control, and whose power has vastly increased in the subsequent
seventy years. It is certainly not self-evident that the central institutions of political democracy are, in their present forms, well
designed to play their central role in a democratic polity and
society.

There is thus a clear case for reform and change, more or less
radical according to different diagnoses, in the very area of political
institutions and conventions where the principle of democracy is
allowed and claimed to be operative. But, as Mill once wrote:

> A democratic constitution, not supported by democratic institutions in
> detail, but confined to the central government, not only is not political
> freedom, but often creates a spirit precisely the reverse, carrying down
> to the lowest grade in society the desire and ambition of political
> domination.[10]

Outside the area of formal government, with some notable exceptions among voluntary organizations and trade unions, in which
principles of election and accountability do operate, there is almost
everything to do, not only in creating democracy, but in establish-
ing that democracy is the principle that ought to operate. Certainly
there may be situations and organizations for which the democratic

principle is inappropriate. That is something that can be argued
over in specific instances. But what is certain is that the democratic
principle – that people should, as far as possible, make or participate in making the decisions that affect them most closely and
importantly – could beneficially be applied far more widely in
modern societies than it presently is. And it would have to be if
those societies seriously aimed at being democratic.

There are other developments, at the international level, which
also provide a challenge to democracy, and may even be taking us
away from it. Within the developed, and generally democratic
world, supranational institutions have emerged which possess great
powers, and are accepted as legitimate by governments, but are in
fact unelected and largely unaccountable bodies.

It may be that some disingenuous economists would suggest that
the International Monetary Fund and the World Bank are purely
economic institutions, lending money to indigent governments
according to strictly economic and commercial criteria. But once
again the falsity of the supposed distinction between the economic
and the political is exposed. The terms on which these unelected
bodies give aid to elected governments are as much political as
economic, and often have the most fateful political and human consequences. How is the make-and-break political power of these
institutions compatible with the operations of democracy at the
national level?

The accountability of the institutions of such important multi-
and supranational organizations as the European Union and the
North American Free Trade Agreement is, to say the least,
minimal. The weakness of the European Parliament in relation to
the European Commission and its many subsidiaries is notorious.
It seems clear that very little thought or energy has been put into
the development of democratic, accountable and elected institutions at the supranational level at which, increasingly, in both the
public and the private spheres, many of the most important and far-
reaching political decisions are being taken. We need global and
supranational democracy as much as, if not more than, we need
democracy at the national and subnational levels.

The outlook for democracy is, therefore, far from being as rosy
and beneficent as has often been suggested in recent years. And it
is further complicated by the recent resurgence of militant Islam.
In some respects contemporary Islam simply follows the traditional
pattern of all theistic religions – which are at one in proclaiming

that the will of God should take precedence over any and every human inclination, decision and policy. The laws of God are supreme, and ought to be embodied and reflected in the laws which govern human society. No human decision or law, whether made by a single ruler or by a popular vote, should be allowed to violate the divine edict; nor would it be legitimate or binding if it did. This is the view taken by Christian fundamentalists, whether Catholic or Protestant, as much as by strict and zealous Muslims. Christian fundamentalists view abortion as murder, and think that the law should therefore prohibit it. Some of them are even prepared to murder doctors and nurses who carry out abortions.

The Muslim fundamentalists believe similarly that secular governments should respect and enact the will of Allah. Those that fail to do so, whether elected or not, forfeit legitimacy. Such an approach to government offers an obvious challenge to democracy, and in Iran in particular we can see a profound struggle taking place between Islamic fundamentalism and democratic tendencies. The situation is further exacerbated by the resentment of Western, and especially American, global dominance which has so powerfully fuelled the Islamic revival. Democracy is a Western product, and induces much the same suspicion as Coca-Cola and McDonaldization. And the failure successfully to export parliamentary systems of government to much of Africa only serves to show how insensitive Western democracies have been to the need to develop models and styles of democracy which are likely to take and find acceptance in non-Western cultures.

There are thus several very formidable threats and challenges to democracy, at both the national and international levels, which will have to be confronted if the democratic principle is to develop and flourish. It is hard to be confident that these challenges will be successfully met, given the strength and dynamism of the forces ranged against it.

Half a century ago the great historian and wise commentator on contemporary events, E.H. Carr, published a series of broadcast talks called *The New Society* (long since out of print). In it he argued that 'mass democracy', as opposed to the old liberal democracy of the nineteenth century, was what the age needed, but it had not yet been created. To my mind his words still offer an all too appropriate warning against complacency and self-congratulation. Democracy remains an ongoing project rather than a safe, secure achievement:

To speak today of the defence of democracy as if we are defending something which we knew and had possessed for many decades or many centuries is self-deception and sham . . . The criterion must be sought not in the survival of traditional institutions, but in the question where power resides and how it is exercised. In this respect democracy is a matter of degree. Some countries today are more democratic than others. But none is perhaps very democratic, if any high standard of democracy is applied. Mass democracy is a difficult and hitherto largely uncharted territory; and we should be nearer the mark, and should have a far more convincing slogan, if we spoke of the need, not to defend democracy, but to create it.[11]

Creating and expanding democracy, which exists under growing threat from the vastly increased activities of non-accountable 'private' conglomerations of power, remains the central task for serious democrats.

# Notes

## Chapter 1

1 Francis Fukuyama, *The End of History and The Last Man*, London, Hamish Hamilton, 1992, and see his article reprinted from the *Wall Street Journal* in *The Independent*, 11 October 2001.
2 *Ibid.*, pp. 49–50.
3 C.B. Macpherson, *The Real World of Democracy*, Oxford, Clarendon Press, 1966, Chapters 2 and 3.
4 *Ibid.*, p. 1.
5 Harley Granville-Barker, *Plays: One*, London, Methuen, 1993, p. 132.

## Chapter 2

1 Aristotle, *The Politics*, 1290b. In the Penguin edition this passage appears in Book III, Ch. 8, but other translations order the text differently.
2 See J.K. Davies, *Democracy and Classical Greece*, London, Fontana, 1978, pp. 35–6.
3 Aristotle, *The Athenian Constitution*, trans. John Warrington, London, Dent Everyman, 1959, pp. 247–9.
4 Thucydides, *The Peloponnesian War*, trans. Rex Warner, Harmondsworth, Penguin Books, 1954, pp. 134–5.
5 Aristotle, *The Athenian Constitution*, p. 270.
6 This point has been made by Peter Green, *The Shadow of the Parthenon*, London, Maurice Temple Smith, 1972, p. 20, and by Ellen Meiksins Wood and Neil Wood, *Class Ideology and Ancient Political Theory*, Oxford, Basil Blackwell, 1978, p. 64.
7 M.I. Finley, *Aspects of Antiquity*, Harmondsworth, Penguin Books, 1972, pp. 60–73, 'Socrates and Athens'.
8 Quoted in M.I. Finley, *Democracy Ancient and Modern*, London, Chatto & Windus, 1973, p. 90.

9 A.H.M. Jones, *Athenian Democracy*, Oxford, Basil Blackwell, 1957, 1977 edn, p. 105.
10 Euripides, *The Suppliant Women*, in *Orestes and Other Plays*, trans. Philip Vellacott, Harmondsworth, Penguin Books, 1972, pp. 206–7.
11 Plato, *Protagoras*, in *Protagoras and Meno*, trans. W.K.C. Guthrie, Harmondsworth, Penguin Books, 1956, pp. 50–51 and 53–4.
12 Wood and Wood, *op. cit.*, p. 15.
13 See, for example, Bernard Crick, *In Defence of Politics*, Harmondsworth, Penguin Books, 1964, Ch. 3, 'A Defence of Politics against Democracy'.
14 See Aristotle, *Politics*, Book I, Ch. 2.
15 Thucydides, *op. cit.*, pp. 118–19.
16 Peter Green, *A Concise History of Ancient Greece*, London, Thames & Hudson, 1973, p. 79.
17 See J.K. Davies, *op. cit.*, p. 69.
18 A.H.M. Jones, *op. cit.*, pp. 5–10.
19 Perry Anderson, *Passages from Antiquity to Feudalism*, London, New Left Books, 1974, p. 43.

**Chapter 3**

1 Quoted in Christopher Hill, *Change and Continuity in Seventeenth-Century England*, London, Weidenfeld & Nicolson, 1974, p. 182.
2 The quotations from Luther are taken from George H. Sabine and Thomas L. Thorson, *A History of Political Theory*, New York, Holt-Saunders, 1973, p. 388; and from *Luther's Works*, Philadelphia, Fortress Press, Vol. 46, 1967, ed. Robert C. Schultz, p. 35, and Vol. 44, 1966, ed. James Atkinson, p. 132.
3 Quoted in Christopher Hill, *op. cit.*, p. 191.
4 François Hotman, *Francogallia*, ed. Ralph E. Giesey, Cambridge, Cambridge University Press, 1972, p. 401. Further page references in brackets are to this edition.
5 *Vindiciae contra Tyrannos*, translated as *A Defence of Liberty against Tyrants*, ed. H.J. Laski, London, Bell, 1924, p. 122. Further page references in brackets are to this edition.
6 George Buchanan, *De Jure Regni apud Scotos*, London, Richard Baldwin, 1689, p. 59.
7 Quoted in *Texts Concerning the Revolt of the Netherlands*, ed. E.H. Kossmann and A.F. Mellink, Cambridge, Cambridge University Press, 1974, pp. 216–17.
8 Quoted in Perry Anderson, *Lineages of the Absolutist State*, London, New Left Books, 1974, p. 50.
9 A.L. Morton, *Freedom in Arms*, London, Lawrence & Wishart, 1975, pp. 30 and 50.

10 Quoted in A.S.P. Woodhouse, *Puritanism and Liberty*, London, J.M. Dent, 1938, p. 89. All the following quotations from the Putney debates are taken from this edition, page references in brackets.

11 C.B. Macpherson, *The Political Theory of Possessive Individualism*, Oxford, Clarendon Press, 1962. For my criticisms of Macpherson's view of the Levellers see 'Revolution, the Levellers and C.B. Macpherson' in Francis Barker *et al.*, *Literature and Power in the Seventeenth Century*, Colchester, University of Essex, 1981, and the further references there.

12 Don M. Wolfe, ed., *Leveller Manifestoes of the Puritan Revolution*, New York, Thomas Nelson, 1944, p. 113.

13 See *ibid.*, p. 269.

14 Geraint Parry, *John Locke*, London, George Allen & Unwin, 1978, p. 96.

15 John Locke, *Second Treatise of Government*, in *Two Treatises of Government*, ed. Peter Laslett, Cambridge, Cambridge University Press, 1960.

16 Macpherson, *Political Theory of Possessive Individualism*, pp. 247–51.

17 Basil Willey, *The Seventeenth Century Background*, London, Chatto & Windus, 1934, p. 240.

18 Quoted in J.P. Kenyon, *Revolution Principles*, Cambridge, Cambridge University Press, 1977, pp. 48–9.

19 Quoted in H.T. Dickinson, *Liberty and Property*, London, Weidenfeld & Nicolson, 1977, p. 128.

20 *Ibid.*, pp. 88–9.

21 See Kenyon, *op. cit.*, pp. 181–2 and 203.

22 Quoted in J.H. Plumb, *England in the Eighteenth Century*, Harmondsworth, Penguin Books, 1950, p. 94.

23 Edmund Burke, *Reflections on the Revolution in France*, Harmondsworth, Penguin Books, 1968, p. 141, and see also pp. 287 and 291. Further page references in brackets are to this edition. 'The tyranny of the multitude . . .' is from a letter of 26 February 1790.

24 See C.B. Macpherson, *Burke*, Oxford, Oxford University Press, 1980, pp. 22 and 48.

25 Quoted in Sabine and Thorson, *op. cit.*, p. 524.

26 Quoted in Christopher Hill, *The Century of Revolution*, Edinburgh, Thomas Nelson, 1961, p. 309.

27 Bernard Mandeville, *The Fable of the Bees*, ed. Philip Harth, Harmondsworth, Penguin Books, 1970, p. 294.

**Chapter 4**

1 E. Weekley, quoted in Raymond Williams, *Culture and Society 1780–1950*, London, Chatto & Windus, 1959, p. xiv.

2 Thomas Paine, *Common Sense*, Harmondsworth, Penguin Books, 1976, p. 67.

3 Quoted in Elisha P. Douglass, *Rebels and Democrats*, Chapel Hill, University of North Carolina Press, 1955, p. 153.

4 See *ibid.*, p. 54.

5 Richard Hofstadter, *The American Political Tradition*, London, Cape, 1962, p. 28.

6 Thomas Jefferson, *Notes on the State of Virginia*, in *The Portable Thomas Jefferson*, ed. Merrill D. Peterson, Harmondsworth, Penguin Books, 1977, p. 164.

7 Richard B. Morris, ed., *Alexander Hamilton and the Founding of the Nation*, New York, Harper Torchback edn, 1969, pp. 154 and 152.

8 Quoted in V.L. Parrington, *Main Currents in American Thought*, Vol. I, New York, Harcourt Brace, 1927, p. 317.

9 Morris, *op. cit.*, p. 131.

10 See *The Federalist*, ed. Max Beloff, Oxford, Basil Blackwell, 1948, p. 366.

11 *Ibid.*, p. 43.

12 The Abbé Sieyès, *What is the Third Estate?*, ed. S.E. Finer, London, Pall Mall, 1963. Further page references in brackets are to this edition.

13 Byron, *Selected Prose*, ed. Peter Gunn, Harmondsworth, Penguin Books, 1972, p. 111. Further page references in brackets are to this collection.

14 Quoted in J.H. Burns, 'J.S. Mill and Democracy, 1829–61', in *Mill*, ed. J.B. Schneewind, London, Macmillan, 1969, p. 290.

15 W.L. Guttsman, ed., *A Plea for Democracy*, London, MacGibbon & Kee, 1967, p. 177.

16 See Mary P. Mack, *Jeremy Bentham*, London, Heinemann, 1962, pp. 432 and 413–16.

17 Quoted in Robert Eccleshall, ed., *British Liberalism*, London, Longman, 1986, p. 149.

18 James Mill's *Essay*, Macaulay's critique of it and the subsequent debate are brought together in *Utilitarian Logic and Politics*, ed. Jack Lively and John Rees, Oxford, Clarendon Press, 1978, p. 59. Further page references in brackets are to this edition.

19 Thomas Paine, *Rights of Man*, Harmondsworth, Penguin Books, 1984, p. 180.

20 Quoted in Eccleshall, *op. cit.*, p. 119.

21 John Stuart Mill, *Autobiography*, ed. Jack Stillinger, London, Oxford University Press, 1971, p. 102. Further page references in brackets are to this edition.

22 J.S. Mill, *On Liberty*, ed. Gertrude Himmelfarb, Harmondsworth, Penguin Books, 1974, p. 62. Further page references in brackets are to this edition.

23 Quoted in Joseph Hamburger, *Macaulay and the Whig Tradition*, Chicago, University of Chicago Press, 1976, p. 134.

24 See Burns, *op. cit.*, p. 323, and Mill, *Autobiography*, pp. 153–4 and 184.
25 Quoted by Burns, *op. cit.*, p. 294.
26 The first statement is quoted in Asa Briggs, *Victorian People*, Harmondsworth, Penguin Books, 1965, p. 209; the second in John Vincent, *The Formation of the Liberal Party*, London, Constable, 1966, p. 187.
27 Quoted in Briggs, *op. cit.*, p. 250.
28 Crick, *In Defence of Politics*, p. 67; see also R.R. Palmer, 'Notes on the use of the word democracy – 1789–1799', *Political Science Quarterly*, Vol. LXVIII, 1953.
29 Mussolini is quoted in Adrian Lyttleton, ed., *Italian Fascisms*, London, Cape, 1973, pp. 49–50.
30 William Kornhauser, *The Politics of Mass Society*, London, Routledge & Kegan Paul, 1960, p. 277. Further page references in brackets are to this edition.
31 Walter Lippmann, *The Public Philosophy*, New York, Mentor Books, 1956, p. 17. Further page references in brackets are to this edition.
32 Crick, *op. cit.*, p. 69.
33 Raymond Aron, 'Social Structure and the Ruling Class', *British Journal of Sociology*, Vol. I, 1950, p. 9.
34 See Williams, *op. cit.*, p. 299.
35 Joseph Schumpeter, *Capitalism, Socialism and Democracy*, London, George Allen & Unwin, 1943. Further page references in brackets are to this edition.
36 The first statement is quoted in Finley, *Democracy Ancient and Modern*, p. 12. For the second, see S.M. Lipset, *Political Man*, London, Heinemann, 1960, p. 32.
37 Edward Shils, *The Torment of Secrecy*, London, Heinemann, 1956, p. 226.
38 W.H. Morris-Jones, 'In Defence of Apathy', *Political Studies*, Vol. II, 1954, p. 37.
39 See Anthony Arblaster, *The Rise and Decline of Western Liberalism*, Oxford, Basil Blackwell, 1984, p. 329 and the accompanying notes.

**Chapter 5**

1 Jean-Jacques Rousseau, *The Social Contract*, trans. Maurice Cranston, Harmondsworth, Penguin Books, 1968, p. 141.
2 J.S. Mill, *Representative Government*, in *Utilitarianism, On Liberty and Representative Government*, London, J.M. Dent, 1976, p. 217.
3 See Jack Lively, *Democracy*, Oxford, Basil Blackwell, 1975, pp. 13, 17–18 and 24.
4 Jeremy Bentham, *An Introduction to the Principles of Morals and Legislation*, Ch. 1, para. 4. This is to be found in most selections from Bentham's writings.

5 Fred Hirsch, *Social Limits to Growth*, London, Routledge & Kegan Paul, 1977, pp. 5 and 10.
6 See Anthony Arblaster, 'The Proper Limits of Pluralism' in Iain Hampsher-Monk, ed., *Defending Politics, Bernard Crick and Pluralism*, London, British Academic Press, 1993, pp. 97–111.

**Chapter 6**

1 See the argument presented by Robert Paul Wolff in *In Defense of Anarchism*, New York, Harper Torchbacks, 1976, especially Part Two. He also includes a reply to one of his critics.
2 Report in *The Guardian*, 29 August 1986.

**Chapter 7**

1 Robert Paul Wolff, *The Poverty of Liberalism*, Boston, Beacon Press, 1968, p. 137.
2 Thomas Carlyle, *Selected Writings*, ed. Alan Shelston, Harmondsworth, Penguin Books, 1971, p. 198.
3 H.H. Wilson, *Pressure Group*, London, Secker & Warburg, 1961, provides a revealing account of this particular campaign.
4 Hugh Brogan, *Tocqueville*, London, Collins Fontana, 1973, p. 30.

**Chapter 8**

1 *Edmund Burke on Government, Politics and Society*, ed. B.W. Hill, Glasgow, Fontana, 1975, pp. 157–8.
2 Aneurin Bevan, *In Place of Fear*, London, Quartet Books, 1978, p. 35.
3 D.H. Lawrence, 'Democracy', in *Selected Essays*, Harmondsworth, Penguin Books, 1950, p. 78.
4 See Wolff, *In Defense of Anarchism*, pp. 34–7.

**Chapter 9**

1 Paine, *Rights of Man*, pp. 41–2.
2 A.D. Lindsay, *The Essentials of Democracy*, London, Oxford University Press, 1929, p. 31. Further page references in brackets are to this edition.
3 Hans Magnus Enzensberger, 'The Industrialization of the Mind', in *Raids and Reconstructions*, London, Pluto Press, 1976, p. 7.
4 Salman Rushdie, *The Jaguar Smile*, London, Pan Books, 1987, p. 36.
5 Graham Greene, *Getting to Know the General*, Harmondsworth, Penguin Books, 1985, pp. 34–5, and also pp. 56–8.
6 Graham Greene, 'Return to Cuba', in *Reflections*, Harmondsworth, Penguin Books, 1991, pp. 217–18.

**Chapter 10**

1 Quoted in Asa Briggs, *The Age of Improvement*, London, Longman, 1959, p. 245.
2 Gavriil Popov, 'Dangers of Democracy', *New York Review of Books*, Vol. XXXVII, No. 13, 16 August 1990.
3 R.H.S. Crossman, *Diaries of a Cabinet Minister*, Vol. I, London, Hamish Hamilton and Cape, 1975, p. 366, and see also p. 414.
4 George Monbiot, *Captive State*, London, Pan Books, 2001, p. 17.
5 See *ibid.*, pp. 331–7, and Chapter 2 'Hospital Cases – the Corporate Takeover of the National Health Service'.
6 Mr Gorbachev's speech was reported at length in *The Guardian*, 2 February 1987.
7 See *The Observer*, 8 March 1987, and the letter from Ian Mikardo MP in *The Observer*, 15 March 1987.
8 See Raymond Williams, *Towards 2000*, London, Chatto/Hogarth, 1983, p. 36.
9 Harold J. Laski, *Democracy at the Crossroads*, London, NCLC Publishing Society, n.d. (but *c.*1934), p. 17.
10 J.S. Mill, *Principles of Political Economy*, Books IV and V, ed. Donald Winch, Harmondsworth, Penguin Books, 1970, p. 314.
11 E.H. Carr, *The New Society*, London, Macmillan, 1951, p. 76.

# Bibliography

To produce a short booklist on a subject which has been passionately debated, on and off, for the past two and a half thousand years is an invidious task. I have simply compiled a list of books which I have found useful. Some omissions are deliberate, but I have undoubtedly also left out many excellent books, which, were I familiar with them, I would have been happy to include. I have also not listed the classic texts mentioned in the body of the book, such as Plato's *Protagoras*, Locke's *Second Treatise*, Rousseau's *Du Contrat Social*, Paine's *Rights of Man*, and so on. Some of the books listed could very well feature in more than one category.

*General*
Bobbio, N. (1990) *Liberalism and Democracy*. London: Verso.
Carr, E.H. (1951) *The New Society*. London: Macmillan.
Duncan, G. (ed.) (1983) *Democratic Theory and Practice*. Cambridge: Cambridge University Press.
Finley, M.I. (1973) *Democracy Ancient and Modern*. London: Chatto & Windus.
Forster, E.M. (1951) *Two Cheers for Democracy*. London: Edward Arnold.
Graham, K. (1986) *The Battle of Democracy*. Brighton: Wheatsheaf Books.
Held, D. (1987) *Models of Democracy*. Oxford: Polity Press.
Hobson, J.A. (1934) *Democracy*. London: John Lane the Bodley Head.
Lawrence, D.H. (1950) Democracy, in *Selected Essays*. Harmondsworth: Penguin Books.
Lindsay, A.D. (1929) *Essentials of Democracy*. London: Oxford University Press.
Lindsay, A.D. (1943) *The Modern Democratic State*. London: Oxford University Press.
Lively, J. (1975) *Democracy*. Oxford: Basil Blackwell.
Lucas, J.R. (1976) *Democracy and Participation*. Harmondsworth: Penguin Books.

Macpherson, C.B. (1966) *The Real World of Democracy*. Oxford: Clarendon Press.

Macpherson, C.B. (1973) *Democratic Theory*. Oxford: Clarendon Press.

Macpherson, C.B. (1977) *The Life and Times of Liberal Democracy*. Oxford: Oxford University Press.

Pateman, C. (1970) *Participation and Democratic Theory*. Cambridge: Cambridge University Press.

Singer, P. (1973) *Democracy and Disobedience*. Oxford: Clarendon Press.

Thompson, D. (1970) *The Democratic Citizen*. Cambridge: Cambridge University Press.

Williams, R. (1983) *Towards 2000*. London: Chatto & Windus/Hogarth Press.

Wolff, Robert Paul (1970) *In Defense of Anarchism*. New York: Harper & Row.

*Classical Greek Democracy*

Davies, J.K. (1978) *Democracy and Classical Greece*. London: Fontana.

Finley, M.I. (1972) *Aspects of Antiquity*. Harmondsworth: Penguin Books.

Forrest, W.G. (1966) *The Emergence of Greek Democracy*. London: Weidenfeld & Nicolson.

Green, P. (1972) *The Shadow of the Parthenon*. London: Maurice Temple Smith.

Jones, A.H.M. (1957) *Athenian Democracy*. Oxford: Basil Blackwell.

Rodewald, C. (ed.) (1975) *Democracy, Ideas and Realities*. London: J.M. Dent.

*The Modern History of Democracy*

Arblaster, A. (1984) *The Rise and Decline of Western Liberalism*. Oxford: Basil Blackwell.

Briggs, A. (1954) *Victorian People*. London: Odhams.

Burnell, P. and Calvert, P. (eds) (1999) *The Resilience of Democracy*. London: Frank Cass.

Dickinson, H.T. (1977) *Liberty and Property*. London: Methuen.

Douglass, E.P. (1955) *Rebels and Democrats*. Chapel Hill: University of North Carolina Press.

Foner, E. (1977) *Tom Paine and Revolutionary America*. London: Oxford University Press.

Gooch, G.P. (1927) *English Democratic Ideas in the Seventeenth Century*. Cambridge: Cambridge University Press.

Hill, C. (1974) *Change and Continuity in Seventeenth-Century England*. London: Weidenfeld & Nicolson.

Hobsbawm, E.J. (1962) *The Age of Revolution*. London: Weidenfeld & Nicolson.

Hobsbawm, E.J. (1975) *The Age of Capital*. London: Weidenfeld & Nicolson.

Hofstadter, R. (1962) *The American Political Tradition*. London: Cape.
*Ideas and Beliefs of the Victorians* (1949) London: Sylvan Press.
Kenyon, J.P. (1977) *Revolution Principles*. Cambridge: Cambridge University Press.
Lively, J. and Lively, A. (eds) (1994) *Democracy in Britain: A Reader*. Oxford: Blackwell.
Lynd, S. (1969) *Intellectual Origins of American Radicalism*. London: Faber.
Moore, B. (1967) *Social Origins of Dictatorship and Democracy*. Harmondsworth: Allen Lane.
Morton, A.L. (ed.) (1975) *Freedom in Arms*. London: Lawrence & Wishart.
Petegorsky, D.W. (1940) *Left-wing Democracy in the English Civil War*. London: Victor Gollancz.
Williams, R. (1959) *Culture and Society 1780–1950*. London: Chatto & Windus.
Woodhouse, A.S.P. (ed.) (1938) *Puritanism and Liberty*. London: J.M. Dent.

*The Contemporary Debate on Democracy*
Aron, R. (1968) *Democracy and Totalitarianism*. London: Weidenfeld & Nicolson.
Bachrach, P. (1969) *The Theory of Democratic Elitism*. London: University of London Press.
Barry, B. (1970) *Sociologists, Economists and Democracy*. London: Collier-Macmillan.
Beetham, D. and Boyle, K. (1994) *Introducing Democracy*. Cambridge: Polity Press.
Benn, T. (1981) *Arguments for Democracy*. London: Cape.
Bottomore, T.B. (1964) *Elites and Society*. London: C.A. Watts.
Crick, B. (1962) *In Defence of Politics*. London: Weidenfeld & Nicolson.
Dahl, R. (1956) *A Preface to Democratic Theory*. Chicago: University of Chicago Press.
Dahl, R. (1982) *Dilemmas of Pluralist Democracy*. London: Yale University Press.
Fukuyama, F. (1992) *The End of History and The Last Man*. London: Hamish Hamilton.
Kornhauser, W. (1960) *The Politics of Mass Society*. London: Routledge & Kegan Paul.
Lippmann, W. (1956) *The Public Philosophy*. New York: Mentor Books.
Lipset, S.M. (1960) *Political Man*. London: Heinemann.
McCoy, C.A. and Playford, J. (eds) (1967) *Apolitical Politics*. New York: Thomas Y. Crowell.
Mernissi, F. (1993) *Islam and Democracy*. London: Virago.

Miliband, R. (1982) *Capitalist Democracy in Britain*. Oxford: Oxford University Press.

Monbiot, G. (2000) *Captive State, The Corporate Takeover of Britain*. London: Macmillan.

Schumpeter, J. (1943) *Capitalism, Socialism and Democracy*. London: George Allen & Unwin.

Spitz, D. (1965) *Patterns of Anti-democratic Thought*. New York: Free Press.

Talmon, J.L. (1952) *The Origins of Totalitarian Democracy*. London: Secker & Warburg.

Williams, R. (1982) *Democracy and Parliament*. London: The Socialist Society.

Wolff, R.P. (1968) *The Poverty of Liberalism*. Boston: Beacon Press.

# Index

Adams, John, 39
Allende, President Salvador, 75
Aristophanes, 18
Aristotle, 15–16, 17, 18, 19, 23, 39, 73, 75
Aron, Raymond, 50
Athenian democracy, 15–25, 59, 85

Bentham, Jeremy, 40, 43–4, 45, 63, 74
Bevan, Aneurin, 80
Bodin, Jean, 29
Bright, John, 47
Bryce, James, 43
Buchanan, George, 28, 29
Burke, Edmund, 8
  on popular tyranny, 41
  on property rights, 34–5
  on representation, 50, 60, 79–80
  on the 'swinish multitude', 38, 49
Byron, George Gordon, Lord, 42

Calvin, John, 27
Carlyle, Thomas, 45, 73
Carr, E.H., 107–8
Castro, Fidel, 93
Chartists, 47, 81, 90, 96
class and class struggle, 16, 24, 38–9, 45, 47, 66, 96
Cleisthenes, 17

Cobbett, William, 42, 96
consent, 49, 68, 86–9, 91, 92
  Locke on, 32–3, 88
Crick, Bernard, 49, 51
Cromwell, Oliver, 30, 31, 32
Crossman, R.H.S., 98

Dahl, Robert, 52, 76
Defoe, Daniel, 34
Diderot, Denis, 35–6
'direct' democracy, see under participation
Disraeli, Benjamin, 8

egalitarianism, 24–5, 41–3, 98–9
  see also inequality
elite theory, 46, 49–50, 52, 60
Enzensberger, Hans Magnus, 91
Euripides, 21–2, 24

Finley, M.I. (Sir Moses), 19
Fox, Charles James, 34, 35
Fox, Henry, 34
freedom, 22, 34, 46, 67, 89–92
Fukuyama, Francis, 1–2

Gallie, W.B., 6
Gentile, Giovanni, 48
Gladstone, William Ewart, 47
Gorbachev, Mikhail, 103

Gordon, William, 38
Granville-Barker, Harley, 8
Green, Professor Peter, 18
Greene, Graham, 93

Hamilton, Alexander, 39, 60
Hardwicke, Lord, 34
Hazlitt, William, 45
Hickes, Dean, 36
Hirsch, Fred, 64
Hitler, Adolf, 3
Holbach, Paul Henri, Baron de, 36
Hotman, François, 28, 29

inequality, 21–2, 35–6, 40, 73, 75–8
  *see also* egalitarianism
interest, the common or general,
  24, 40, 51, 63–5, 72–5
Ireton, Henry, 30, 31, 32

Jefferson, Thomas, 38–9
Jones, A.H.M., 25

Kornhauser, William, 49, 51

Laski, Harold, 105
Lawrence, D.H., 82
Levellers, 26, 30–2
liberty, *see* freedom
Lindsay, A.D., 89, 91, 92, 105
Lippmann, Walter, 49
Lipset, Seymour Martin, 51
Lively, Professor Jack, 63
Locke, John, 32–4, 67, 88
Lowe, Robert, 47
Luther, Martin, 27

Macaulay, Thomas Babbington,
  Lord, 45, 46
Macpherson, C.B., 3, 7, 31, 33
Madison, James, 40, 60
majority, alleged tyranny of, 22, 35,
  41, 46, 89
Mandeville, Bernard, 36

Marcos, Ferdinand, 3, 53
Marx, Karl and Marxism, 91, 95–6
Miall, Edward, 45, 47
Michels, Roberto, 49
Mill, James, 44, 45, 60
Mill, John Stuart, on Athenian
  democracy, 19
  on 'the common herd', 49
  doubts about democracy, 45, 89
  on participation, 61, 105
  on rule by public opinion, 43, 46,
    60
  on rule by the wisest, 39, 46, 49
  'mob', fear of the, 7, 15–16, 25,
    29–30, 34, 36, 42, 45, 49, 52
Monbiot, George, 99
Morton, A.L., 30
Mosca, Gaetano, 49
Mussolini, Benito, 48

Nicaragua, democracy in, 3–4, 93
Northern Ireland, 5, 6, 67, 68–9, 76

Ortega, President Daniel, 93
Overton, Richard, 31–2

Paine, Thomas, 42, 44
  on popular sovereignty, 87
  on representative democracy, 38,
    44, 60, 79, 81
Pareto, Vilfredo, 49
Parliament, accountability to, 4–5
  and the Levellers, 30, 31–2
  and J.S. Mill, 46
  non-elected chamber of, 4, 104
  property and, 34–5
  representation and, 79–83
  sovereignty of, 60, 82, 104
  Whigs and, 34
participation, 19–21, 23–4, 25, 38,
  51–2, 60–1, 63, 79, 82, 84–5,
  93–4
Pericles, 8, 18, 23, 24, 60
Petty, Maximilian, 30

Plamenatz, John, 52, 77
Plato, 8, 18, 19, 21, 22, 37, 46
pluralism, 40, 51–2, 65, 72, 73–4,
    76–7
Popov, Gavriil, 97
property (and political rights),
    30–6, 38–40
Protestantism, 26–7
Putney debates (1647), 26, 30–1

Rainborough, Thomas, 31
referenda, 38, 82, 84–5, 86
representation, advantages of,
    39–40, 60
  in Britain, 4–5
  Burke on, 34–5, 80
  claims to, 10
  Greeks and, 25
  nature of, 79–83
  size and, 44, 79
Rousseau, Jean-Jacques, 25, 40
  and freedom, 59–60, 67
  and the general interest, 40–1,
    64–5, 74–5, 80
  and inequality, 75
  and popular sovereignty, 60, 87
  and smallness, 40–1, 53
Rushdie, Salman, 93

Saint-Simon, Claude-Henri, 45
Schumpeter, Joseph, 50–1
Sexby, Edward, 30–1

Shils, Edward, 51
Sieyès, Abbé, 41, 66
Socrates, 18–19, 21, 22
Solon, 16–17
sovereignty, popular, 28–9, 30, 32,
    61, 82, 104
Soviet Union, 1, 3, 97, 103

Thatcher, Margaret, 8, 100
Thucydides, 18, 23
Tocqueville, Alexis de, 9, 43, 45,
    48, 78, 89
Torrijos, General Omar, 93
Tyrrell, James, 34

Utilitarianism, 43–4

Voltaire, François-Marie Arouet
    de, 36

Weekley, Ernest, 37
Wesley, John, 34
Wildman, John, 31
Willey, Basil, 34
Williams, Raymond, 104
Wilson, President Woodrow, 48
Wolff, Robert Paul, 67, 73
women, exclusion from
    democracy of, 24, 31, 41, 46,
    78, 96–7
Wordsworth, William, 41–2

**FEMINISM**

**Jane Freedman**

- What is the relevance of feminist thought to today's society?
- What do feminists mean by equality and difference?
- Can we find unity in feminist thought, or only conflict?

*Feminism* provides an introduction to some of the major debates within feminist theory and action. Focusing on the perennial question of equality and difference, the book examines the way in which this has been played out in different areas of feminist social and political theory. Jane Freedman adopts a refreshing approach by focusing on issues rather than schools of thought. Among the subjects she examines are politics and women's citizenship, paid and unpaid employment and the global economy, sexuality and power, and race and ethnicity. Finally, the book analyses the problem of essentialism for feminism and the challenge of postmodern and poststructuralist theories. Written in a jargon-free style, this book presents a clear and concise introduction to a wide range of feminist thought.

*Contents*
*Introduction: Feminism or feminisms? – Equal or different? The perennial feminist problematic – Feminism and the political: the fight for women's citizenship – Employment and the global economy – Sexuality and power – Ethnicity and identity: the problem of essentialism and the postmodern challenge – Bibliography – Index.*

112pp    0 335 20415 5 (Paperback)    0 335 20416 3 (Hardback)

# DISCOURSE

**David Howarth**

- What do we mean by discourse?
- What are the different conceptions of discourse and methods of discourse analysis in the contemporary social sciences?
- How can this concept help to clarify key theoretical problems and illuminate empirical cases?

The concept of discourse provokes considerable debate and is understood in a variety of ways in the contemporary social sciences. This text presents a comprehensive overview of the different conceptions and methods of discourse analysis, while setting out the traditions of thinking in which these conceptions have emerged. It surveys structuralist, post-structuralist and post-Marxist theory, and the author sets out a fresh approach to discourse analysis, drawing principally on the writings of Saussure, Lévi-Strauss, Gramsci, Althusser, Foucault, Derrida, Laclau and Mouffe. He evaluates a number of pertinent criticisms of this approach, and explores ways in which discourse analysis can assist our understanding of identity formation, hegemony, and the relationship between structure and agency. This concise and engaging text provides a stimulating introduction to the concept of discourse for students and researchers across the social sciences.

## Contents

*Introduction: defining the concept of discourse – Saussure, structuralism and symbolic systems – Post-structuralism, deconstruction and textuality – Foucault's archaeology of discursive practices – Genealogy, power/knowledge and problematization – The limits of ideology in marxist theory – Laclau and Mouffe's theory of discourse – Deploying discourse theory – References – Index.*

176pp    0 335 20070 2 (Paperback)    0 335 20071 0 (Hardback)

## CULTURE
## REINVENTING THE SOCIAL SCIENCES
**Mark J. Smith**

- How has the meaning of culture been reconsidered?
- What impact has this had on approaches to social enquiry?
- Should culture be seen as central to social science?

Over the past three decades there has been a transformation in the ways that social science has been conducted. In order to understand what is happening, we have to explore the implications of a rethinking of the meaning of culture, from a hierarchical system of classification to a contested space. This wide-ranging introduction to the concept of culture examines the ways in which we approach social enquiry, and argues that cultural theory can help to overcome problems in disciplinary and interdisciplinary analysis. Mark J. Smith explores how changes in the meaning of 'culture' have pinpointed key shifts in the way we research society, and draws on contemporary sociology, psychology, politics, geography and the study of crime to consider the ways in which cultural transformation has changed the landscape of social research. He concludes with a persuasive and focused discussion of the centrality of culture in post-disciplinary social science. This landmark text represents essential reading for students and researchers with an interest in the cultural dimension of social science.

### Contents
*Prologue: culture and the postdisciplinary imperative – A genealogy of culture: from canonicity to classification – Culture and everday life: the ordinary is extraordinary – Culture and structure: the logic of mediation – Culture and hegemony: towards the logic of articulation – Contested cultural spaces: identity discourse and the body – Culture and the prospects for a postdisciplinary social science – References – Index.*

c144pp    0 335 20318 3 (Paperback)    0 335 20319 1 (Hardback)